ON
BOWIE
ROB SHEFFIELD

HEADLINE

First published in Great Britain in 2016
by HEADLINE PUBLISHING GROUP

First published in paperback in 2017
by HEADLINE PUBLISHING GROUP

1

Cataloguing in Publication Data is available from the British Library

Paperback ISBN 978 1 4722 4107 8

Typeset in 11.4/18.32 pt Stempel Garamond LT Std by Jouve (UK)

Printed and bound in Great Britain by Clays Ltd, St Ives plc

Headline's policy is to use papers that are natural, renewable and recyclable
products and made from wood grown in sustainable forests.
The logging and manufacturing processes are expected to conform
to the environmental regulations of the country of origin.

HEADLINE PUBLISHING GROUP
An Hachette UK Company
Carmelite House
50 Victoria Embankment
London EC4Y 0DZ

www.headline.co.uk
www.hachette.co.uk

For Sarah and Allison, Charlie and David,
Sydney and Jackie, Mallory and Maggie

CONTENTS

The man replied, "Things as they are
Are changed upon the blue guitar."

—Wallace Stevens, "The Man with the Blue Guitar"

INTRODUCTION

1

Planet Earth is a lot bluer without David Bowie, the greatest rock star who ever fell to this or any other world. He was the hottest tramp, the slinkiest vagabond, the prettiest star who ever shouted "You're not alone!" to an arena full of the world's loneliest kids. He was the most human and most alien of rock artists, turning to face the strange, speaking to the freak in everyone. He stared into your twitchy teenage eyes to assure you that you've torn your dress and your face is a mess, yet that's precisely why you're a juvenile success. Whichever Bowie you loved best—the glam starman, the wispy balladeer, the Berlin archduke—he made you feel braver and freer, which is why the world felt different after you heard Bowie. This man's spaceship always knew which way to go.

That's why he always inspired such fierce devotion. As a teenager in the eighties, at home glued to my radio on a Saturday night because I couldn't get a ticket to the Serious Moonlight tour in Boston, I listened as a group of WBCN DJs arrived at the studio fresh from the show, with a cigarette butt they swiped from the man's ashtray backstage. And I listened with goose bumps as they ceremonially smoked it on the air. Bowie fanatics are like that. Which is why so many different people have heard themselves in his music, whether it's Barbra Streisand covering "Life on Mars?" in 1974 or D'Angelo covering "Space Oddity" in 2012, George Clinton name-checking him on *Mothership Connection* or Public Enemy sampling him in "Night of the Living Baseheads." Somehow I really thought he'd outlive us all. After all, he'd outlived so many David Bowies before.

The weekend he died, I was listening to nothing but Bowie. On Friday night, his birthday, I went to see the tribute band Holy Holy play *The Man Who Sold the World* in New York, with his longtime producer Tony Visconti on bass, original Spiders drummer Woody Woodmansey, and Heaven 17 singer Glenn Gregory. After finishing the album, they did another solid hour of early-seventies Bowie classics from "Five Years" to "Watch That Man." Visconti had the crowd sing "Happy Birthday" into his phone and texted it to Bowie. "David's at his birthday party," he told us. "This isn't it." (Were we all secretly hoping maybe the Dame would show up? Of course we were.) I got weepy when Visconti's daughter sang "Lady Stardust," a song that has always made me verklempt because it reminded me Bowie was going to die someday, though Friday night, that still seemed far away. I spent the rest of the weekend listening to *Station to Station* and *Low*—an ordinary weekend, since those are easily the two most-played albums in my apartment— along with the 1974 outtake "Candidate (Demo)," and of course the new *Blackstar*, an album that sounded very different before Sunday night.

As Visconti said after the news broke, *Blackstar* was a "parting gift." In his last couple of years on the planet, Bowie threw himself back into the music career everyone figured he'd gracefully retired from, making *The Next Day* and *Blackstar* as his farewells to the flock he'd assembled over the years. Heading for the final curtain, Bowie chose to face it the way he faced everything else—it was cold and it rained, so he felt like an actor and went to work, going out at a creative peak. No other rock artist has left a final testament anything like this. Nor like the bizarre yet excellent off-Broadway musical he debuted last year, *Lazarus*, which I was lucky enough to see in December— definitely the only time I've ever seen actors sing "'Heroes'" while swimming like dolphins through a puddle of milk.

The whole world was stunned by the news of his death on January 10—just two days after he celebrated his sixty-ninth birthday by dropping his newest masterwork, *Blackstar*. The album was a surprise in itself—he just announced it last November, presenting the ten-minute title song out of the blue—and its release inspired a worldwide outpouring of Bowie love. What none of us knew—except Bowie—was that this was the end. He'd just been diagnosed with cancer, and knew by November it was terminal. But he had plans for the music he wanted to make in the time he had left. While the world was still toasting Bowie's latest creation, the news came that he'd died quietly at home, surrounded by his family. Ever the innovator, Bowie found a new way to wave bye-bye and say good night, moving on to his next phase as the late, great David Bowie, teaching us how to hear his old records in different ways. A new career in a new town.

This book is a love letter to Bowie, a celebration of his life and his music. It's a thank-you for the beautiful mess he made out of all our lives. It's the story of how he changed my world and yours. It's a reflection on what he means today and why his death hit us so hard. It's a travelogue following the fantastic voyage of an artist who spent fifty years looking for new ways to surprise and challenge our sense of what was possible. It's a gallery of the faces he showed us. It's a toast to the just-for-one-day we got to share with him. And it's also a love letter to everyone who adored him, because bringing us together is what he was really all about. Let's celebrate each other by celebrating him.

2

For all his spaciness, it was his crackpot compassion that made him Bowie. The lust for human connection is what his music is all about. That's why the hero of "Starman" isn't the actual starman—it's the two kids who talk about him, after picking up his signal on the radio. ("I had to phone someone so I picked on you—hey that's far out, so you heard him too?") The starman just shows up to give them an excuse to bond, a secret they can hide from their parents (who'd have them locked up if they knew). Bowie did that for all of us who loved him. He was the cracked pastor, shepherding his flock of lost kids. Many a lifelong friendship has begun in that "so you heard him too?"

Bowie's mission was bringing these misfits and loners and freaks together. That's why listening to Bowie sent you back to your drab daylight world with fresh eyes, noticing all the glamour of ordinary people in ordinary places. Transition. Transmission.

You can see that compassion even in a movie like *The Man Who Fell to Earth*, which barely has a single coherent scene. The movie is a mess, just because Bowie is too hot to share the screen with anyone—you can see all the other actors watching him, wondering, "Is David looking at me? Does he think I'm pretty? Does he respect my creative process?" Everyone gets so dazed and distracted by his presence, nobody gets around to making a movie. Bowie's at his most zonked out, yet he looks so cool (orange hair! Borsalino hat! trench coat and tennis whites and silver pants!) that I've seen this movie several dozen times anyway. As the alien stranded on earth, Bowie records an album, *The Visitor*, for his wife back on his home planet, hoping it will get played on the radio and his wife out there in space will hear it.

That music—we never hear it in the movie—might be the hazy cosmic jive Bowie hears on the radio in "Starman," the 1972 hit that made him a sensation in the UK after years of false starts. The best portrait of Bowie in the 1970s remains the BBC documentary *Cracked Actor*, where he twitches, sniffles, sings along with Aretha Franklin in the back of his limo, and does his onstage Hamlet-in-shades routine, holding a skull in his hand and jamming his tongue down its throat. Suck, baby, suck. He hit Number 1 in the U.S. with the disco John Lennon collabo "Fame," which got instantly plundered by James Brown for "Hot (I Need To Be Loved, Loved, Loved)"— making Bowie the rare rock star who could claim James Brown ripped *him* off. (Shortly before he died, the Godfather said that if he ever had a tribute album, Bowie would be his choice to do "Soul Power"—one of the weirdest things JB ever said.) His "plastic soul" period culminated at the 1975 Grammy Awards, where Bowie, looking dashing but scarily drug-ravaged in his tux, greeted the crowd: "Ladies and gentlemen—and others." He gave the Best R&B Vocal Performance, Female, trophy to

Aretha, who gushed, "Wow, this is so good, I could kiss David Bowie! I mean that in a beautiful way, because we dig it!"

Yet Bowie was just hitting his golden years, rushing out his five best albums from 1976 to 1980, the best five-album run of anyone in the seventies (or since): *Station to Station*, *Low*, *"Heroes,"* *Lodger*, and *Scary Monsters*. In this time span, he also made the two albums that brought back Iggy Pop from the dead—*The Idiot*, prized by Bowie freaks as a rare showcase for his eccentric lead guitar, and *Lust for Life*—and his finest live album, *Stage*, from the 1978 tour, absurdly turning the ambient instrumentals from *Low* and *"Heroes"* into arena rock. As he put it at the time, "I'm using myself as a canvas and trying to paint the truth of our time on it. The white face, the baggy pants—they're Pierrot, the eternal clown putting across the great sadness of 1976."

The eighties were a whole decade of Bowies. He took over MTV with *Let's Dance*, moving in on the New Romantic pop he'd created in his own image. After a decade or so in the wilderness, he began writing strong songs again in the late nineties, with *Earthling* and *Hours*, discovering what became the grand theme of his final phase—true love, the kind he'd found with Iman. He explored that theme through the excellent albums of his final years: *Heathen*, *Reality*, *The Next Day*, and *Blackstar*. Though he dropped out of sight in the late 2000s, his mystique just grew. When he released new music, it was because he had a reason; when he didn't, that was also for a reason. The world was happy to play by Bowie's rules.

3

"I've lived all over the world / I've left every place," Bowie boasted on *Low*, which he released in January 1977, the week he turned thirty. He was just a vagabond back then, playing up his role as the lodger slipping from town to town, station to station, in search of his next musical disguise. He kept that wanderlust his entire life. He was the artist as fan, cheerfully presenting himself as an anthology of selves, a human mix tape listening to the world and echoing back his favorite bits, combining them into something new.

"I don't want to climb out of my fantasies to go up onstage," he told *Rolling Stone* in 1971. "I want to take them onstage with me." He made no pretense to rock naturalism, speeding through his roles before they had a chance to get stale. He was always willing to risk the unknown, even if that meant falling on his face. (Dude took decades of mockery for "The Laughing Gnome" and, honestly, deserved every bit of it.) He made spectacular disasters a central part of his artistic statement, embracing every possible way he could find to make himself ridiculous, up to and including performing under a giant glass spider. Nobody enjoyed laughing at his humiliations more than he did, as in his comment on the 1974 *David Live*: "God, that album! I've never played it. The tension it must contain must be like a vampire's teeth coming down on you. And that photo on the cover. My God, it looks as if I've just stepped out of the grave. That's actually how I felt. That record should have been called *David Bowie Is Alive and Well and Living Only in Theory*."

There probably isn't a Bowie fan on earth who can claim to like *all* his different phases—not even Bowie himself. But whichever Bowie was your favorite, he (or she) had elements in common with the others. "The reinvention thing—I don't buy into that at all," he said in 1997. "I think there's a real continuity with what I do and that's expressing myself in a contemporaneous fashion. The reinvention thing, it's an easy description, isn't it? 'Hey Dave, you're a real chameleon!' 'I'm probably the chameleon of rock because what I do is all ch-ch-changes!'"

Well said. (And with that, the clichés "chameleon" and "reinvention" go back to the attic where they belong.) He's right— that's just not adequate as a vocabulary for everything Bowie achieved, the way he used all these sounds and visions to act out the loves and hates and passions of his music. That's what made him such a bizarre influence who shows up all over our culture. The mystery of whether Thomas Pynchon heard "Space Oddity" before writing the last hundred pages of *Gravity's Rainbow* is one of those questions I never stop asking myself.

Like anyone who moves fast, he was dangerous to trust. He

always had detractors who questioned his authenticity, doubted he was in it for the music. When *Uncut* magazine in June 2008 asked Keith Richards to pick his favorite Bowie song, he replied, "Can't remember. Who is he? Oh, he went to the same art school as me. 'Changes,' maybe. That's about it. Not a large fan, no. It's all pose. It's all fucking posing. It's nothing to do with music. He knows it, too."

Bowie needed to provoke this kind of reaction—in the game he was playing, it would have been an artistic failure if nobody hated him for being a fake. (And you have to cut Keith some slack for poseur-phobia, given that he's spent his whole life a few inches from Mick.) In 1979, right around the time hip-hop started making noise in New York, Bowie was comparing himself to a DJ, telling his life story by digging in the crates of his record collection: "I am a DJ, I am what I play." ("DJ," of course, were also David Jones's initials.) So it's understandable that some people would dismiss him as a contrived fraud. But he warned us from the start, in "Five Years": life is short, so add as many personalities for your collection as you can. The whole world is a box of pinups for you to ransack. I'd like to be a gallery, put you all inside my show.

4

Scene: It's 1976, and David Bowie is alive and well and living only in a theory called L.A. He has a new album coming out in a few weeks—*Station to Station*, he calls it—and he's decided to give it a world premiere on TV. Not some glamorous prime-time event, but on *Dinah!*, a syndicated morning kaffeeklatsch that airs before the Bowies of the world get out of bed, hosted by daytime-TV lifer Dinah Shore. It's the debut of the Thin White Duke, and it's a magnificent performance, as if he's inspired by his down-market surroundings—Bowie has never moved better, strutting his stuff to "Stay" in an electric-blue outfit.

After "Stay," he sits for an interview. Bowie is remarkably relaxed and polite, compared to his other zonked-out TV appearances at the time. Maybe it's because Dinah's an old-school showbiz trouper, or maybe just because he deeply respects her audience of day-drinking American housewives. The other guests on Dinah's couch are 1970s TV stars Nancy Walker and Henry Winkler, giving Bowie the chance to gush, "I'm a great fan of Fonzie."

Unlike some of the other TV people he encounters these days, Dinah isn't trying to compete with him hipness-wise—she represents an Old Hollywood tradition Bowie respects a lot more than he respects the rock machine. Dinah asks him to comment on a photo where he's wearing his outsize pantaloons from the Philly Dogs tour. Bowie explains, "I'd been living in New York for some time, so I was wearing a lot of Puerto Rican clothing."

Dinah—pleasant and laid-back as always, with her exaggerated southern drawl—is intrigued. "There is no set costume?" she asks. "So you're influenced by whatever you like at the moment?"

Bowie nods. "It tends to be like that, yes. I'm easily saturated. I'm very sort of faddy, sort of flirty. I'm quite a rock fan—I get influenced by other bands, other artists, and I tend to sort of steal things from them."

Dinah smiles. "You're being very modest." Bowie replies, "Not at all, no. I think that's one of the most important elements of rock and roll."

Bowie looks more colorful than ever, a swirl of neon orange hair atop his blue shirt, contrasting with Dinah's pale gray couch. He's giving top-notch Bowie Worldview right now, but the really astounding thing about this conversation is how calm and thoughtful he is about it. It's a rare treat to see Bowie look someone in the eye. He likes talking rock clobber with an old American broad—the forties singer who did "Buttons and Bows." Dinah's a pro. She knows what "I am what I play" means.

Dinah: "You give *so much* of yourself!"

Bowie: "No, not really."

Bowie liked to wear sexy pop trash on the outside because sexy pop trash was how he felt on the inside. Glam, as he always said, had nothing to do with actual fashion. "Glam wasn't like that at all. It was Woolworth's. Woolworth's posing as Jean

Genet. The ideal collision of vulgarity and high-mindedness."
Glam, as Bowie defined it, was a way of perceiving the world
around you, as a first step toward remaking it, so it was key to
wear things that had credibility as trash. Any kid could copy
the look, and that was the point. Glam was a style of pop devotion, wearing your fandom on your sleeve, dressing yourself up
in satin-and-tat scraps that straight types would throw away. It
meant wearing broken pieces of the things that inspired you,
the way Catholics display icons as emblems of the divine.

The pop devotion Bowie told Dinah about was real, because
he never stopped being a fan—if Bowie loved your music, he
wouldn't shut up about it. He'd make you a star, as he did with
Lou Reed and Iggy Pop—the first thing he did when he blew
up was produce hit records for his obscure idols, at a time when
he had his hands full building his own career. If you were a
nobody with a new sound, he'd lure you into your spotlight,
whether you were Luther Vandross or Stevie Ray Vaughan
or Adrian Belew. He loved to sponsor upstart bands, out of
sincere enthusiasm—he loved the Polyphonic Spree quite a bit
more than anybody else did then or now, and doted on them
faithfully long after their hipness bubble had burst. There was
a period in the early 2000s where you couldn't see a band in
town without Bowie making his grand entrance. When Television were first playing at CBGB in the early 1970s, he gave
them a blurb to use on gig fliers. ("The most original band I've

seen in New York. They've got it.") It wasn't that he had un-erring taste—how would that ever be the point?—but he had the appetite of a true pop fan. His last album was inspired by Kendrick Lamar, who was born during the Glass Spider tour.

Unlike your average rock god, Bowie was not stuck up about embracing his imitators—he loved it when the future leg-ends ripped him off, because that was the realest flattery for the original rip-off king. He relished his role as the mother of the House of Bowie. There were exceptions—for some reason, he had an ax to grind against poor Gary Numan, and always seemed a degree or two frosty on the subject of Elton John. But he made an unannounced appearance onstage with Morrissey to sing T. Rex's "Cosmic Dancer," in 1991, at a sold-out Forum in Los Angeles—the footage is remarkable because it's the only time in Morrissey's life that he's looked sincerely humbled. When Bowie walks out, Moz just gives the warmest smile, re-duced (at his own show!) to a helpless fan, unable to feel any-thing but the most innocent kind of pleasure. (And that was pretty much it for Morrissey's career as a smiler.)

Whether he was paying his respects to his influences or his disciples, he gave the ultimate compliment: he kept stealing from them. Roll the dice and steal the rice. When he came back with *Let's Dance*, he showed off the moves he'd been copping from all the bands he'd influenced, like Duran Duran and ABC and Spandau Ballet—for new wave kids like me, it was incredibly flattering to realize that Bowie wanted in on our action. Us? He's listening to *us*? He wants a touch of *our* glimmer?

Pop stardom, the way he defined it, means you keep feeling fascination for the now sound right up to the moment—you don't settle for what you did yesterday. You tune in to the pop trash all over the radio dial for any ideas worth scavenging. You loot the past and smuggle it into the future, whether that means Otis Redding stealing a Bing Crosby song, or Jay Z and Kanye West stealing the same song from Otis Redding, or David Bowie stealing every song from pretty much everybody ever. At this point, everybody listens to pop the way Bowie always listened, which is: this is cool, how can I *steal* it?

5

He made his most flamboyant bow on *Top of the Pops* with "Starman," strumming his blue guitar—four minutes of glam that changed the world. Virtually every kid who saw this performance went on to start a band. I always loved this line from Ian McCulloch of Echo and the Bunnymen, in 1984: "I thought, 'Where's he from? He definitely can't live in Beckenham.'" It set a whole new standard for interstellar sex-druid posturing. As Oasis's Noel Gallagher said, "When I saw Bowie on *Top of the Pops* I thought he came from Mars. I was disappointed when I found out he was called Jones and came from Battersea."

He was the biggest self-proclaimed phony the rock world had ever seen. It was no coincidence that he was also the first self-proclaimed gay rock star. As he announced in 1972, "I'm gay and always have been, even when I was David Jones." He proclaimed he met his wife Angie "while we were laying the same bloke."

When he draped his arm around Mick Ronson for the BBC "Starman," homosexuality had only been decrimimalized in the UK a few years earlier. (Five years, as it happens.) The scientific minds of the American Medical Association classified homosexuality as a mental disorder until 1973. (It took them until *Aladdin Sane*?) Bowie performed his gay identity in public as opposed to in bed, where his costars tended to be women, quiet as he kept that. In "Five Years," he sees a queer on the street, just another pedestrian in his welcome-to-my-world panorama of humanity. As Boy George said, "I remember hearing 'Five Years' for the first time. That song was quite important because, prior to that, the word 'queer' was always something you heard in the school playground. It wasn't said in an affectionate way. So hearing that in a song, it was like, 'Wow, someone's actually using that language in music.'"

The seventies were full of gay rock stars who were officially closeted. Strange as it sounds now, Freddie Mercury vehemently denied being gay until 1991—the week he died. Elton John married a woman in the eighties. It's hard to say with any certainty how much of Bowie's gay bravado was showbiz; none of that obscures the fact that Bowie was walking point for queer rock fans at a time when this simply wasn't done. It was a revelation for kids like Morrissey, who got his first look at Bowie on *Top of the Pops* and decided, "There was no doubt that this was fantastically homosexual." By the time the Smiths started, Morrissey boasted he'd seen Bowie in concert sixteen times. "He would roll into Doncaster or Bradford in 1972, looking as he did, and if you had a problem with it, then it was your problem—not his—he was the one who was always laughing or smiling. He wasn't persecuted by anything. It was the people who objected who were persecuted." Bowie invited anyone to rebel against hetero conformity. Gender roles were just homework to throw onto the fire.

No other rock star presented sex so playfully, as so free of macho resentment, so devoid of power tripping, so inclusive, so pervy, so funny. When he wrote an "All the Young Dudes" for the boys, he also wrote a "Rebel Rebel" for the girls, yet anyone in his audience could hear themselves in both songs. He faced sex with an Ovid-like sense of constant mutation. He sang about the transformative power of desire, the way it warped his body and soul, which is why he attracted his own breed of young folk going through that difficult phase. He came to give us something extravagant to dream on, and we liked him that way. "I needed him to be big because I was so little," Karen O of the Yeah Yeah Yeahs once told me. "I didn't have his records, but I didn't need to because he was always there. Make a wish and Bowie's there."

No star was ever so committed to the idea that all of us who listened to him, or who got it, or who were just cool—we were all beautiful because of our flaws, not in spite of them. As everyone knows, Bowie's eye was injured and nearly blinded in a schoolyard scuffle—he got punched in the eye, suffering traumatic mydriasis that permanently dilated his left pupil and impaired his vision. His eyes were two different colors because of that injury, something anyone could see right away. But he played that up, to the point where it seemed gauche and lame to have "normal" eyes. The karaoke principle: if you can't fix it, flaunt it. It makes all the sense in the world that the kid who punched him (over a girl—Bowie cheerfully admitted he deserved it) was George Underwood, who not only remained a lifelong friend, but became a key visual collaborator, as an artist working on Bowie's album covers and stage sets. When Bowie answered reader questions for Q magazine, somebody asked what he'd say to the kid who injured his eye. Bowie replied, "See you at dinner, George." That was a key part of the Bowie cosmology: the scars on your skin are something to brandish, like the ones on your soul. As he sang in "Win," "Wear your wound with honor, make someone proud."

6

Hard as he tried sometimes to keep people from noticing, it was always the music that came first with Bowie. He got thoroughly steeped in R&B during his apprenticeship—no matter how far he got into other genres, he had that rock and roll twitch he picked up from his years in London clubs leading cover bands, singing James Brown and Bo Diddley and John Lee Hooker songs for rowdy crowds. That was the foundation of everything he did, which gave him an edge over so many of his admirers. Before he ever began composing wispy folkie ballads, he had sung "Land of a Thousand Dances" and "Duke of Earl" and "I Wish You Would" during countless late nights in front of pill-popping, pint-swilling punters who were there to dance and drink and fight. He quit his first band because they refused to cover Marvin Gaye's "Can I Get a Witness."

The London mod club scene where he earned his stripes as a performer that was Bowie's Hamburg, his schooling in the R&B essentials, where he learned to keep a step ahead of the crowd and make sure the kids on the floor were already working up a sweat before the first purple heart kicked in. So many Bowie imitators failed to get to first base because they just couldn't match his sense of forward motion. And however far he journeyed into more rarefied musical realms, he always remained clearly a guy who'd learned his shit from James Brown. Even the Berlin albums are structured on the classic R&B model—

fast ones on the A-side, slow ones on the flip side. And he never stopped diddling around with the sax. As he said in 1993, "I'm told I have the technique of Bill Clinton, but I believe I play with the enthusiasm of Coltrane."

"It was just the songs and the trousers," Bowie said in 2002. "That's what sold Ziggy. I think the audience filled in everything else." But great as his trousers were, it was the songs that turned the trick, because Bowie's concept of himself as a rock star demanded songs that were better than anyone else's, which Bowie had the ambition and invention to write, even though it took him years to get the hang of it. Like Oscar Wilde, who lamented, "I find it harder and harder every day to live up to my blue china," Bowie chose such ambitiously gaudy trousers because he knew they'd challenge him to keep proving himself worthy. He made every aspect of his performance—the lyrics, the stagecraft, the album cover, the video—part of his statement, and then moved on to the next one, leaving a trail of masterpieces and catastrophes, experiments that paid off and haircuts that didn't, dabbling in every art form he could scam his way into whether he had any knack or not.

Yet everything that made Bowie my hero—it's all there in "Young Americans," from 1975, a song of almost bottomless compassion. He belts it in his tortured Elvis voice, a pushing-thirty limey rock star full of yearning and affection (and lust, lots of that) for the young Americans he sees around him. He wishes he could be as real and openhearted as they are, yet he can't, partly because he's old and English, but mostly because he's that poseur who calls himself David Bowie. Yet he admires these kids and envies their messy feelings—those kids *are* the song that makes him break down and cry. Especially the two lovers on the road, all the way from Washington, who pose a question anyone can relate to: "We've lived for just these twenty years—do we have to die for the fifty more?" Bowie's answer was no, and he proved it—he kept expanding and mutating right up to the edge of seventy, celebrating his sixty-ninth birthday with an album that lived up to the restless spirit he'd chased his whole career. He assured his fans we didn't have to give up on life, didn't have to play it safe, didn't have to fall into a rut—and he proved it was possible in his own music. (If he says he can do it, he can do it—he don't make false claims.) He kept inventing new worlds just for the pleasure of changing them. And in doing so, he changed our world as well.

THE NIGHT
DAVID BOWIE DIED

2016

I was up late at my desk, writing. I got a text at 1:43 A.M. from a friend who'd just been over for dinner a few hours earlier to watch the Golden Globe Awards. "Did you see the news"—that's never good. I texted her back "what happened" with one hand while googling "death" with the other. News had just come over, and it was bad news. I knew I wasn't going to be sleeping that night. I thought about waking up my wife to tell her. But I wanted her to sleep one more night in a world that had Bowie in it.

I pressed play on the tape that was already in the boom box next to my desk, "Bowie Mix 00." A driving tape, geared toward songs that sounded good in the car. Side A starts with "Five Years" and ends with "Scary Monsters"; side B starts with "Aladdin Sane" and ends with "A New Career in a New Town." The tape has taken a battering over the past sixteen years, but it still plays. As the "Five Years" drums faded in, I thought of all my friends who were sleeping through this, wishing I could protect them from the news, hoping they'd sleep as long as possible. I started writing my memorial tribute for *Rolling Stone*. I traded e-mails with insomniac friends. It was still early on the West Coast, so I went online to see what Kanye had to say, and it was morning in England, so I looked at what Gary Numan had to say—just two of the countless artists Bowie taught me how to hear. The whole Internet had already turned into a Bowie shrine. It was like that scene in "Five Years"—getting the news, wandering in search of some kind of human connection and finding it in unexpected places. Suddenly you're surrounded by all these people going through the same shock and grief you feel, all of our heads hurting like a warehouse. Never thought I'd need so many people.

I learned a lot about Bowie that night and in the days that followed—I don't know why I'd be surprised that he'd keep teaching me things, even after his death, but he did. It was a massive outpouring of grief, bigger than anyone could have guessed. He was even more widely beloved than I'd realized, because every culture and every generation had its own Bowie. The moment turned into a global funeral like nothing else we've seen in recent years. None of the rage that surrounded John Lennon's death when I was a kid—just overwhelming gratitude for his life. It was an Irish wake around the world. As my aunt Eileen in Dublin would say, we put him down well.

No rock star of his stature had died like this—a couple of days after releasing a masterpiece on his sixty-ninth birthday. This wasn't anything like Kurt or Biggie or D. Boon or Aaliyah, who died young and tragically. This was an old man who'd used his time. We'd all just seen him beaming in the birthday photo Iman published on Friday—dapper in his suit, no socks, fedora at a jaunty angle. I'd had countless conversations about Bowie in the previous days—everyone I knew was in the midst of the global birthday celebration, as we absorbed *Blackstar*. At the Holy Holy tribute show that Friday night, everybody in the crowd kept buzzing about the new album—so warm, so jazzy, so bittersweet. One of his ten best. That was already clear by Friday night or Saturday afternoon. And then came late Sunday night.

I put on *Blackstar*. This was clearly his farewell. I'd been listening to this music nonstop for a few days already, but now it sounded utterly different—tonight it sounded like an album by a man at the end of a long and full life, refusing any self-pity, still wishing he had more time, singing over and over, "at the center of it all, your eyes." (As another one of his creations sang years ago, on his way to a similar exit, "Tell my wife I love her very much.") The man who sang these songs had lived a life, and had worked hard to learn how to fall in love with the world he was about to leave.

I flipped through an old issue of a British music magazine

with Bowie on the cover—I have whole shelves of those—a magazine I happened to buy the night I met my wife for the first time. It was February 2003 in Charlottesville: I was meeting friends for dinner at Baja Bean; I was a couple of hours early; I went next door to Plan 9 Records and bought a rock mag so I could read it over some nachos in a booth by myself. A few hours later, I was face-to-face with the woman of my future. (New love, a boy and girl are talking.) She was an astrophysicist and a goth Bowie freak—quite a combo. On one of our first dates in NYC, I took her to the New School, where I was giving a lecture on Bob Dylan. She didn't have anything to add to the discussion. She told me afterward, "Bowie is my Dylan. Bowie is also my Bowie."

Bowie was always a rock star who told me the truth. He warned me love was a scary monster and he was right. Love is *not* loving—it wants to tear you apart and rip your sense of identity to shreds and lead you astray and get you mixed up with people from bad homes. You can hide from it, but alas, that doesn't work. It's been tried—by Bowie, for one, a man who spent much of the seventies and eighties freeze-drying his synapses with any chemical within reach, only to accidentally bump into true romance with (of all people) a model. He fell in love at first sight. She didn't. As he said, "I was naming the children the night we met." Iman was harder to impress. "I fell in love with David Jones," she said. "Bowie is just a persona.

David Jones is a man I met." She probably met the real David Jones long before Bowie himself did.

When he dropped out of sight in his sixties, after a 2004 heart attack, fans figured he'd finally slipped away to the private life he deserved, and that he'd found a clever way to retire discreetly. It was a shock on January 8, 2013—again on his birthday, this one his sixty-sixth—when he announced a new album that hadn't been rumored about by even the most obsessive Bowie watchers, the masterful *The Next Day*. And it was another shock when he returned with *Blackstar*—a completely different album, more of an R&B flow with goth guitar. (It says a lot about Bowie that he was able to make these albums without anyone finding out—it says something about his guile, but it says more about the loyalty he inspired. Nobody breathed a word.) For some reason he had more stories he wanted to tell us, both musically and vocally. He also had some secrets he didn't want to tell yet.

He lived with his cancer diagnosis for eighteen months. ("The whole Ziggy Stardust thing was eighteen months, from beginning to end," Bowie said in 2002. "It was a really short period of time.") He knew his death would make the world lonely, so he did what no other rock star has managed—he made one last masterpiece as a parting gift. This was how he chose to spend his last year on earth? Working? Guess he cared about us more than we even knew. He was already giving us music to help us grieve. Bowie's songs had been a crucial part of my grief experiences, just because he was so attuned to erotic loss—the way the heart keeps suffering through its endless metamorphoses. So it was a new experience to mourn for him. It's hard to let go of David Bowie. (I never wave bye-bye. But I try. I try.)

When I was in my early twenties, I assumed my Bowie fandom was something that had peaked in my teens. That stands to reason, right? Except nothing stands to reason in the Bowie universe—reason kneels before Bowie to lick his finger, then another finger, then his cigarette. And as it turned out, I became far more obsessed with Bowie in my late twenties than before—particularly *Low*, which spoke to my pushing-thirty sense of disillusionment. In my thirties, forget about it—I got more Bowie-mad than I'd ever been. How was I supposed to understand these songs when I was a mere high school boy? When I was thirteen, I loved "DJ" for its tumult of quick-flash sexual confusion: the DJ's alone in his booth, but he's got a girl out there, but he's not sure who she is, maybe she's listening, maybe she's dancing, maybe she doesn't exist, how would he know? I can still remember what I *thought* that song meant to me in my teens . . . but it mattered a lot more when I was older and had lived a life worth getting confused about. How did I never notice "The Secret Life of Arabia" before? Or "Win"? "After All"? "Be My Wife"? "Growing Up and I'm Fine"? Going through adult pain, that gave me a different

Bowie, who tapped into emotional zones I never had access to in high school. The songs kept changing, and so did the listening boy.

As the sun rose on Monday morning, I was still at my desk, still grieving, still writing, still listening. I put on "Where Are We Now?," one of my favorite Bowie songs, his sixty-sixth-birthday present. It's a ballad about moving through time, haunted by the places and faces you've left behind. He murmurs in his crooner mode—a little "Life on Mars?," a little "'Heroes,'" quite a bit of Roxy Music. The question is "Where Are We Now?" and the answer is he doesn't know, and neither do the people he loves. It's a song about not knowing where you are on the timeline—are you halfway through your life? 90 percent finished?—and surrendering to the moment, with all the confusion and fear it entails.

I fell in love with "Where Are We Now?" a few years ago, months after it came out. October 2, 2013: I'm up in New Haven, Connecticut, giving a talk at Yale. I'm sentimental about being back at my alma mater, so I slip out for a late-night stroll. I walk past Toad's Place, a divey rock club I remember well—can't believe this place is still around. I saw so many bands here in the eighties—Hüsker Dü, the Replacements, Iggy, the Pogues. Tonight there's a flier in the window for a tribute act called Wham Bam Bowie Band, playing *Ziggy Stardust* all the way through. So of course I pop in for a song or two. The club is untouched since the eighties—the walls are still painted with giant portraits of Joan Jett and Billy Idol. Wham Bam Bowie Band are just plugging in. Do all sixteen of us paying customers sing along, right to the end of side 2? Do the band speak in English accents even though they're from Asheville, North Carolina? Does the lady at the next table keep yelling for "Width of a Circle"? Yeses all around. Great show—the only tribute band I've ever seen who duplicate the phone ringing at the end of "Life on Mars?"

Then, for the encore, the singer says, "Some of you may know David Bowie released an album this year. We'd like to do a song from the new one," and my gut reaction is, Oh *noooo*. Cover bands never do songs from the new album, even good ones—that's the first rule. Buzzkill. But they begin "Where Are We Now?" and I'm shocked when nobody leaves. None of us can sing the verses, but we can all fake the chorus, at least the second time around. I belt "Where Are We Now?" out loud with sixteen strangers I'll never see again. It's one of the most ridiculously happy moments in my life as a Bowie fan. Then the band plays "Rebel Rebel," and that's cool too. Years later I'm still trying to figure out the joy in that moment. So where *are* we now?

My wife opened the bedroom door and shuffled into the kitchen, a few minutes before seven. She already knew the news. When she woke up to her phone alarm, she noticed she had a dozen messages, all about the same thing. She just said, "I know," and we looked at each other, then made some coffee.

That night, we stood in the living room with the lights out, *Blackstar* on, and looked out at the skyline of New York, his adopted hometown. No stars—just a vast, clear, and empty January sky. The moon was a crescent—the kind of "pleasant crescent moon" Bowie's old pal Marc Bolan liked to sing about, facing down like the one at the start of *2001*. I realized there was no danger of going to sleep in a world without Bowie in it. The way he changed the world—changed how we heard it, how we saw it—was written all over the sky. The stars are never sleeping. Where are we now? As long as there's sun. As long as there's rain. As long as there's you. As long as there's me. Just for one day.

THE LONDON BOY

1947

He was born David Jones in Brixton in 1947, with an elder half brother, Terry, who tutored him in Beat poetry and jazz. He got turned onto music at the age of nine, when his dad brought him home a Little Richard single, "Tutti Frutti." "I had heard God," Bowie said later. In the beginning was the *wop bop a loo bop a wop bam boom*. He took sax lessons from local hero Ronnie Ross. Years later, he repaid Ross by bringing him in to play the sax solo in Lou Reed's "Walk on the Wild Side."

By the age of sixteen, David Jones was already a face in the clubs, playing sax in his first band, the Konrads. He spent years kicking around the London mod scene, making records with his bands the Lower Third, the King Bees, and the Manish Boys. He was mad about clothes. As he recalled, "I lived out of the dustbins on the backstreets of Carnaby." He was broke, so one day his manager sent him to paint the office with another scuffling kid who needed a day's wages. The other kid turned out to be Marc Bolan, the future superstar of T. Rex, then still known as Marc Feld, but who announced himself as King Mod. Bolan looked him over and said, "Your shoes are crap." It was the dawn of a lifelong rivalry.

Like Bob Dylan or Ringo Starr, he picked a stage name that reflected a boyish love of cowboy movies—almost a parody of a London lad's idea of an American name, calling himself after a famous Texan with a signature knife. He needed a new name in a hurry—he was already a pro in January 1966 when his next manager, Kenneth Pitt, cabled from New York with the news that America had a new hit group called the Monkees, with a singer named Davy Jones. Not such an unusual turn of events that another Davy Jones got famous before he did—but the surprise is the other Davy Jones also stayed famous forever, as the Cute One (and resident cheeky Brit) in the Monkees. I'm a lifelong fan of both Joneses, so as a moonage daydream believer, I feel obliged to point out that the name suited the Monkee much better—Bowie was always meant for a flashier handle. Occasionally, their musical paths crossed. Bowie sounds most like Monkee Jones in his 1977 "Be My Wife." (Sometimes you get *so* lonely.) Monkee Jones's Bowie-est moment has to be the amazing 1967 "Star Collector," sneering a Carole King–Gerry Goffin song with a pioneering Moog synthesizer solo and lyrics that conflate space travel with banging groupies.

Tellingly, Bowie never made the move to change his name

legally—he continued to sign his contracts "David Jones." For some reason, he wanted to keep his alter ego of "Jones" around as his secret sharer, the real-life self he could hide in a trunk for safekeeping, like the Bowie doll carried by his backing singers on the famous 1979 *Saturday Night Live* version of "The Man Who Sold the World." For the rest of his life, part of him remained Jones, and the rest remained Bowie. And until he met Iman, at least, he devoted almost all his attention to Bowie, at Jones's expense. In the sixties, his primary objective was getting Bowie as famous as possible. In March 1966, he made it to TV, performing "Can't Help Thinking About Me" on *Ready Steady Go!* "Mr. Bowie, a 19-year-old Bromley boy," according to *Melody Maker*, "writes and arranges his own numbers." A busy lad, he's also helping to compose a musical score, while designing shirts and suits for a Carnaby Street shop. "Also I want to go to Tibet. It's a fascinating place, y'know. I'd like to have a holiday and have a look inside the monasteries. The Tibetan monks, lamas, bury themselves inside the mountains for weeks and only eat every three days. They're ridiculous—and it's said they live for centuries."

Bowie also scared up publicity by leading an organization called the League for the Prevention of Cruelty to Long-Haired Men. It got him into the papers, but not the charts. He talked his way into a juicy tabloid controversy after his hair got him banned from the BBC pop show *Gadzooks! It's All Happening*.

The producer was in on the scam, naturally (he later claimed it was his idea), and provided the press with outraged quotes vowing to cancel the Manish Boys' performance unless the singer trimmed his locks. In the *Daily Mirror*, under the headline, "Row Over Davie's Hair," the artist declared, "I wouldn't have my hair cut for the Prime Minister, let alone the BBC. My girlfriend isn't keen on my hair either. Maybe it's because I get asked for more dates when we're together."

Of course the BBC surrendered at the last minute and the Manish Boys played their new single "I Pity the Fool"—but it bombed anyway. The Manish Boys also scored a gig to open for Bowie's idol James Brown in Portsmouth—but, tragically, the band's van broke down on the way, and he had to settle for getting there in time to catch the headliner. One day, a top London session musician turned him on to grass for the first time. Bowie's cannabis mentor was John Paul Jones, later the bassist of Led Zeppelin. (Jimmy Page played on Bowie's early records as well.) Some of his early tunes had promise—"I'm Not Losing Sleep" and "The London Boys" and "Let Me Sleep Beside You." But as Bowie kept hustling around the fringes of the London music scene, he was starting to look like a professional next big thing with a bright future behind him.

He performed for a while in a folkie troupe called Feathers, with his first girlfriend, Hermione Farthingale. He also got heavily into mime at the Beckenham Arts Lab, studying with another key early mentor, Lindsay Kemp. What he really learned from mime was how to steal. As Kemp put it, "You simply go and see everything, and you nick the good ideas. Then you do it better, simply by using Scotch tape, sawdust and a little imagination." In February 1969, Bowie got some good news: his old nemesis Marc Bolan, now riding high on the charts, invited him to be the opening act on a British tour. The bad news: Bolan hired him as a mime. "Marc was quite cruel about David's as-yet-unproven musical career," his producer Tony Visconti told biographer David Buckley. "I think it was with great sadistic delight that Marc hired David to open for Tyrannosaurus Rex, not as a musical act, but as a mime."

The show must go on. Bowie did his mime pieces *Yet-San and the Eagle* and *The Mask* for the T. Rex fans, dramatizing a Tibetan Buddhist boy's persecution at the hands of the Chinese (years before Tibet became something rockers were supposed to know or care about). "All the Maoists turned up and heckled me, waving their little red books in the air," he recalled in 2002. "Marc Bolan was delighted and thought it an unmitigated success. I was trembling with anger and went home sulking." He had to feel a bit of that Tibetan boy's persecution himself. The indignity of opening for a rock band, right there on that stage, but getting paid *not* to open his mouth. To stand so close to that applause. And none for him. He craved his own taste of that. All he needed was a hit.

MAJOR TOM

1969–1980–2016

TEN

"I must've had over seven hundred singles out before 'Space Oddity,' and half of them were daft as a brush," Bowie once said. Only one became truly infamous—"The Laughing Gnome," an appalling piece of hippie whimsy. ("Gnome man's land," oh dear.) Then one night Bowie got stoned, went to see *2001: A Space Odyssey,* and got inspired to write a ballad about an astronaut named Major Tom who gets very lost in inner space, drifting over the edge of reality and beyond the infinite. It was Bowie's first step into the big time, a space trip complete with a ten-nine-eight countdown and a blastoff. Bowie was now a star. And as HAL 9000 would say, there was something extremely odd about his mission.

NINE

Major Tom is the greatest role Bowie ever played, his most beloved creation. It's a story he kept telling his whole career, from

"TVC15" to "Ashes to Ashes" to "Hallo Spaceboy" to "Blackstar." But it's also a story everybody else wanted to tell—no rock classic inspired so much fan fiction, from Peter Schilling's "Major Tom (Coming Home)" to Lou Reed's "Satellite of Love" to Marvin Gaye's "A Funky Space Reincarnation," so many unauthorized sequels about lonely spaceboys yearning to splash down. Of all Bowie's characters, nobody's lived as many lives as Major Tom.

Bowie identified hard with the tale of the astro boy who got too high and couldn't come down. "A lot of my space creations are, in fact, facets of me," he says in the 1975 *Cracked Actor* documentary. "Major Tom in 'Space Oddity' was something. Aladdin Sane. They were all facets of me. . . . I couldn't decide whether I was writing the characters or the characters were writing me."

"Space Oddity" was a UK hit in the summer of 1969, the same summer as the first moon landing. The radio wouldn't play it, since it was perceived as a gimmick and a novelty in dubious taste—if the astronauts had failed to survive their moon walk, certainly a real possibility, his career would have been over. As Bowie described it proudly at the time, "It's a mixture of Salvador Dalí, *2001*, and the Bee Gees." The obvious template was the Bee Gees' hit "New York Mining Disaster 1941 (Have You Seen My Wife, Mr. Jones?)," another acoustic death soap. (There was no New York mining disaster in 1941, just as there was no Major Tom lost in space.) Apart from the sonic similarities, the Bee Gees' hit is the rare pop song to use iambic pentameter, like "Space Oddity," and of course it features a Mr. Jones who won't get a chance to tell his wife he loves her very much.

So much of his sound is already there in this early phase—the mix of acoustic guitar and electronics, the melodramatic wobble of the harmonies. It takes off from the Beatles' "Baby's in Black," the song that invented Bowie if anything did, and the Rolling Stones' "Something Happened to Me Yesterday"—the line "I'm floating in a most peculiar way" is a straight rip from that song, where Mick Jagger closes *Between the Buttons* by singing a vaudeville rooty-toot about a devastatingly illuminating new experience that will make it hard for him to go back to the life he knew before. Mick could be singing about either psychedelic drugs or gay sex—it depends on whether you think he's singing "something rather trippy" or "something rather drippy." Bowie seems to have decided "both."

"Space Oddity" was his first hit, and Bowie had a hard time hiding how grateful he was to finally get noticed. As he told the *New Musical Express* in November 1969, "I've been the male equivalent of a dumb blonde for a few years, and I was beginning to despair of people accepting me for my music. It may be fine for a male model to be told he's a great-looking guy, but that doesn't help a singer much, especially now that the pretty boy personality cult seems to be on the way out." Bowie hoped it would soon lead to bigger things, with a strange whiff of desperation in his tone. "I throw myself on the mercy of the audience, and I really need them to respond to me. If they don't I'm lost. I'm determined to be an entertainer, clubs, cabaret, concerts, the lot."

All his life, Bowie kept rewriting the tale of Major Tom. In his 1980 sequel "Ashes to Ashes," a Number 1 UK hit, he sings in the voice of Tom as a New Romantic fame junkie, stranded out in space, begging for an ax to break the ice so he can finally fall to earth. "Hallo Spaceboy" was a 1995 synth pop gem from the otherwise dull Eno collaboration *Outside*, spruced up with a twelve-inch Pet Shop Boys remix. Bowie hits a club where he brushes up against a sexy spaceboy on the dance floor. He can't figure this kid out ("Do you like boys or girls?") but he picks him up with the promise "moon dust will cover you," as they dance off into the night together. Yet even in bed, he's singing "Bye bye love," turning the Everly Brothers oldie into Major Tom's kiss-off to the planet. Earth below us, drifting, falling. That's a common melancholy in Bowie songs: things you love rise up to the stars and leave you bereft on the ground. Satellite's gone up to the sky, things like that drive me out of my mind. My baby's in there someplace, rotating in the sky. I will see you in the sky tonight. There's something in the sky, shining in the light. The stars are never sleeping.

That's what's so seductive about the Major Tom fantasy—and that's why there are so many songs about him. You can stay high and remain aloof and shine like a satellite of love, if you're Lou Reed. Or a satellite of hate, if you're Depeche Mode (in "Satellite," from *A Broken Frame*). You can spend the cold day with a lonely satellite, if you're Duran Duran. Or you can just float alone up there for a long long time, if you're Elton John. Elton turned it into "Rocket Man," a gloriously sad ballad in its own right. For some reason, Bowie always seemed to have a bit of side-eye for "Rocket Man," quoting it in his live performances of "Space Oddity." (In the book *Moonage Daydream* he adds, "We didn't exactly become pals, not really having that much in common, especially musically.") Even in 2013 he was still trying to steal his space glitter back from Elton with the excellent B-side "Like a Rocket Man."

Bowie, of course, kept updating the song, too. Until the final days of his life, as he himself realized it was time for him to go blackstar on us: look at me now, I'm in heaven. The "Blackstar" video showed a woman on another planet finding Tom's dead body in his crashed capsule, his skull crowned with jewels. The people of her planet worship Tom's skull as an idol, using its dark powers to torture a couple of human prisoners—one of whom is played by Bowie.

EIGHT

Peter Schilling's "Major Tom (Coming Home)" is the best faux-Bowie rip of all time—not only is it just as famous as "Space Oddity" or "Ashes to Ashes," it's entered the story so fully that it's impossible to filter it out. It's probably the best answer song ever, easily the best fan-fic sequel any artist ever presumed to write to somebody else's hit. Part of the perfection of "Major Tom" is that Peter Schilling, like our astronaut hero, flashed once and then floated weightless into space. You just knew this guy was a one-hit wonder—a handsome Euro synth-disco jet-boy, singing in his touchingly vulnerable quaver of a German accent. Unlike "99 Luftballons," where the German version was the keeper and the English-translation version a footnote, "Major Tom" was better in English—the fact that Schilling was singing in a language that was clearly a challenge for him just added to the ambience of alienated yearning. The radio and MTV were full of Bowie clones in the early eighties—that was part of what made *Let's Dance* so cool, that Bowie was jumping on a real live pop moment he'd begotten in the first place. But this was the most shameless of all.

It was such a weird trick to try—nobody really knew what to make of it. Not even Schilling, who played coy and didn't seem to speak English well at all. I vividly remember an interview on MTV where he told Martha Quinn flat out his song had *nothing* to do with Bowie—his character just happened to have the same name. Even Martha Quinn couldn't believe he was claiming this. I can't believe it either. Was he kidding? You don't lie to Martha Quinn. It just added to the general air of this song as something adults were not supposed to take seriously.

Except there was one adult in my world who did take this song seriously—the pioneering disco critic Mike Freedberg of the *Boston Phoenix*, who not only named this the greatest song of 1983 but wrote an essay explaining why. It was a beautiful poetic mediation on the whole Major Tom saga, exploring the connection between Bowie, disco, and New Romantic synth pop. It blew my mind—an adult, a writer, taking my dipshit teenage pop thrills as seriously as I did. This essay had a pretty major impact on my life—I read it in the school library, a few days before my eighteenth birthday, and it felt like the writer was reading my mind. I copied huge passages of it into my diary. Since it's my favorite thing ever written about Bowie, and since I've never seen it reprinted anywhere, I'll quote a bit of it here—in fact, I happen to be copying directly from my teenage diary, which is balanced here on my knees as I type.

As Freedberg tells the story, Major Tom belongs as much to Schilling as he does to Bowie, because Major Tom belongs to the world of teen romantics. "In 'Space Oddity' (as *Ziggy Stardust* and *Aladdin Sane* showed more clearly) Bowie put together a new kind of lonely loverboy's rock and roll, one that was fussier and more intricate and dressed up with the cosmetics of lyric symbolism and the evening clothes of production." But the grandeur of the music came from a sense of feeling isolated and rejected. "Being a lonely loverboy meant being high above the ground and far, far away from the ground, from mundane potential rivals. As compensation for being lonely, the unloved loverboy generated his own self-esteem; as security against being unwanted, he had his dreams, his imagination—he could make himself desirable, handsome, ineffably lovely. . . . Schilling's Major Tom is a disco space oddity, a distant dream; the more distant he becomes the better he feels. This is his loser's revenge. . . . Major Toms enjoy being misunderstood."

That's why the Major Tom mythos wasn't exactly the healthiest influence on my teen psyche—it flattered my adolescent self-pity, made me think my sense of isolation was a noble achievement rather than a problem that could be solved (or at least contained) with patience and help (and possibly medication). Yet I'm hardly the only Bowie kid who went through this. That's why there are so many Bowie kids out there, with new ones born every day. That's also why there are so many damn songs telling this story.

"Major Tom (Coming Home)" used to be one of my wife's karaoke go-to picks, until she had to retire it after that moment on *Breaking Bad* when the DEA agent finds a karaoke video in the belongings of a murdered drug lord. The dead guy is singing "Major Tom (Coming Home)," and it's so vulnerable and goofy that it's just agony to watch. The men in the room crack up laughing at the video, but Walter White (the high school chemistry teacher who lives a secret life as a meth kingpin) doesn't laugh, especially since he knows all the horrible details about the murder. The dead crook karaokeing "Major Tom" is the same dead crook who gave him that book of Walt Whitman's poetry. Bowie, like Whitman, knows the allure of having a secret life in the night. Bowie, like Whitman, is the poet of lost boys and their fear of being found.

SEVEN

Bowie always heard himself in Tom, which is why he kept checking in on this guy. "Ashes to Ashes" was his way of looking back at the past ten years and asking where it all went wrong. "The second time around there were elements of my really wanting to be clean of drugs," he told *Mojo* in 2002. "I metamorphed all that into the Major Tom character, so it's partially autobiographical. But not completely so: there's a fantasy element in it as well. It probably came from my wanting to be healthy again. Definitely. And the first time around it wasn't. The first time around it was merely about feeling lonely. But then the limpets of time grabbed hold of the hull of my ship; it was de-barnacling by the time I got round to 'Ashes to Ashes.' No, leave all this out, actually, the barnacles . . . Jesus Christ!"

The interviewer notes he's gone a bit Captain Birdseye. "I know. Davy Jones' locker!"

Major Tom works that way for lots of people. He shows up everywhere, usually in disguise. You can hear Bono sing about him in U2's "Bad"—come on down, come on down, all that desperation and separation, the isolation and desolation, why not let it go and come on down? Bono made the connection explicit when he did his famous "Bad" at Live Aid, throwing in "Satellite of Love" and "Walk on the Wild Side." "She could feel the satellite coming down / Pretty soon she was in London Town"—that's a happy-ending version of the story. Joy Division's "Disorder" is a darker version—Ian Curtis really wants to come down, feel the pleasures of a normal man (or is that "another man"?), but he can't find anywhere to land.

Lana Del Rey has a torch ballad called "Terrence Loves You," where she gets trashed listening to the tunes of the rock star who's left her behind, singing, "Ground control to Major Tom, can you hear me all night long?" (The title might be her nod to Bowie's doomed brother Terry.) William Shatner, bless him, did the 2011 concept album *Seeking Major Tom*, full of Shatnerized spoken-word versions of rock songs about outer space, sequenced to narrate Tom's entire life. It has great moments (Sheryl Crow's "Mrs. Major Tom") and not-so-great moments (Captain Kirk declaims "Walking on the Moon").

The unexpectedly poignant finale: Shatner recites the lyrics of Duran Duran's "Planet Earth," then ends with Tom's last message to the world, "I love youuuu."

A remarkably creepy "Space Oddity" was recorded by an anonymous group of 1970s Canadian schoolchildren, whose LP *The Langley Schools Music Project* became a cult item. Bowie praised the Langley version as "a piece of art that I couldn't have conceived of, even with half of Colombia's finest export products in me." The song also inspired notable covers from Cat Power (in a car commercial) and Smashing Pumpkins. But the best cover has to be D'Angelo, on his long-awaited 2012 comeback tour—within minutes of the first gig in Paris, the whole world was YouTubing his "Space Oddity" with our jaws hanging open. After all those years away, lost in his own personal tin can, D'Angelo came back to strum his acoustic guitar and work the hell out of "tell my wife I love her very much" line. Marilyn Manson's "Apple of Sodom" is probably the only variant with the punch line, "I'm dying, hope you're dying too."

Patti Smith's "Distant Fingers" flips the tale from a Jersey-chick perspective, a doo-wop love song to her boyfriend on Mars. (She couldn't find one in Jersey.) On one of her early live bootlegs, from 1975, Patti introduces it with memories of growing up as a duck-footed misfit. "When I was a kid, I didn't have great promise. I didn't get a guy like that. And I didn't get one, and I didn't get one, and I didn't get one. So I said, 'All right, earth boys. You had your chance.' And I started looking up to bluer pastures."

When she sang this song, Patti was just a poet dabbling in rock and roll. A year later, she was a star herself, big enough to visit Bowie backstage when he played the L.A. Forum. She spilled a beer on Angie Bowie's mink. Like Tom's spaceship, this song just keeps going on forever, passing through places it was never intended to go.

SIX

Major Tom speaks his final words to earth: "Tell my wife I love her very much." The Peter Schilling version adds a bit of shade: "Give my wife my love—and nothing more." I have a strange (or not so) identification with Tom's wife, and an alternate timeline in my head where I'm the toddler he left behind with the wife. I think about Tom's wife often, and not just when the song is playing—it would be a completely different tale without her. Where does that "she knows" come from? Is Tom the one who says "she knows" when he sends his love—did he realize how much she loved him and will miss him? Or is "she knows" one of the Ground Control guys trying to talk Tom down? Depends on my mood when I hear it. Did his last words make her grief easier or harder? Did he really say "give my wife my love and nothing more"? Or did he just say "give her my love" before the circuits went dead? Did he mean it when he sent her his love? And does she really know?

There was no real reason for Bowie to give Tom a wife—marriage was still a bit exotic in 1969 rock culture, too adult for the audience. (Bowie wasn't married yet—he and Angie had just met, at a King Crimson press function.) But for some reason, it was important to him. She's the only person in the song who might call Tom by his name instead of his title, the way Iman kept insisting she was married to David Jones. The wife is the only detail Bowie reveals about the life he left behind. She has his love. And nothing more.

FIVE

Bowie's sci-fi caper made him the C-3PO of rock and roll—a golden droid who has adventures all over the galaxy yet remains fussily British (and gay?) wherever he goes, a universal translator fluent in over six million forms of communication. Like any protocol droid, he's programmed to study and copy humans, but he's strictly an interpreter who isn't supposed to have feelings of his own. C-3PO's Bowie-est moment is *Return of the Jedi*, on the planet where he gets worshipped as a rock star. "I do believe they think I am some kind of god," he tells Han Solo. "It's against my programming to impersonate a deity."

Seventies kid culture was obsessed with space travel, which was new at the time and offered a hopeful escape fantasy from the escalating threat of nuclear obliteration. Saturday-morning TV was full of adventures like *Josie and the Pussycats in Outer Space*, *The Lost Saucer*, *Land of the Lost*, and *Far Out Space Nuts*. These were mostly involuntary space-captivity narratives—our heroes get accidentally launched into orbit or fall through a portal. *Far Out Space Nuts* had Bob Denver, a.k.a. Gilligan, as a NASA janitor who accidentally hits the "launch" button instead of "lunch." The Pussycats, a cartoon rock band of three girls dressed as feline sex goddesses, just happened to be visiting a rocket ship for a photo shoot; their manager's pesky sister bumped them onto the launch lever. The story is the same: we didn't *choose* to go to space, it just happened to us. The perfect metaphor for adolescence, especially in the seventies, when the sex-and-drugs frontiers were exploding—the transition into adolescence seemed more drastic and traumatic than ever before, a frontier best crossed as an abduction. It was also a ready-made metaphor for sexual awakening. The idea of being trapped in zero gravity with Josie and her Pussycats was more than my hormonal circuits could handle.

FOUR

One of my favorite Major Tom songs is "TVC15," from the 1976 *Station to Station*. This time, Bowie's girl is the one who trips out to the stars, and he's the one left on earth. She jumps into her TV set, which beams her to a satellite. Now Bowie dances to his TV set all night and wishes he could be with her and spend some time together: "My baby's in there someplace, rotating in the sky." He grinds his teeth and swivels his hips to that New Orleans piano strut. This might be Bowie's most sexually confident vocal, which is saying something. It turns out he likes space girls—it takes the pressure off. The distance gets him hot.

He wasn't the first singer to lose his girl to outer space, of course—Louis Prima's incredible 1957 single "Beep! Beep!" has his baby going to the moon and sending him back bleeps and bloops via Sputnik. He wasn't the first to croon about romance in the sky, either—according to my boyhood copy of *The Guinness Book of World Records*, the world's favorite song was "Stardust," popularized by his eventual Christmas pal Bing "Ziggy" Crosby. But Bowie made this kind of loneliness his own. The only one who can touch him is the rap star Future, who's in a proud tradition of Atlanta hip-hop sci-fi. My favorite Future song is called "Astronaut Chick," where he slobbers in a druggy haze, staring up at the sky with pupils the size of billiard balls, "You're my astronaut chick and that's the only thing that matters to me." Bowie would relate.

THREE

Has any movie inspired rock stars as much as *2001*? "I loved *2001*," Mick Jagger told Rolling Stone in 1968. "A very commercial movie." (A strange compliment, though from Mick Jagger, it's the highest praise.) Everybody stole musical and visual ideas from it, from Zeppelin to Sabbath to Floyd, from T. Rex to Neil Young to the Who. But nobody did more with it than Bowie. In 2009, his son Duncan Jones directed the very strange and very excellent sci-fi film *Moon*, which does for *2001* what Peter Schilling did for "Space Oddity." Sam Rockwell plays an astronaut trapped on the moon for a little too long, with no human contact. It's like everybody's forgotten he's there.

2001 is full of themes close to the Bowie heart—the unspoken secrets between travelers in space, the grief when the only other human around slips into the void, the sense of listening to the silence of space and straining to hear coded messages that aren't there. HAL 9000 even talks like Bowie. The astronauts say, "He acts like he has genuine emotions—he's programmed that way to make it easier for us to talk to him. But as to whether or not he has real feelings is something I don't think anyone can truthfully answer."

That sums up our boy pretty well in 1969. He communicates most comfortably from a distance. That's how he wants us to see him: a rock and roll monolith sending out strange radio emissions, but otherwise emotionally inert—its origin and purpose still a total mystery.

TWO

Planet Earth is blue.

Blue blue electric blue, that's the color of my room. Put on your red shoes and dance the blues. I never did anything out of the blue. Now my Blue Jean's blue. See these eyes so green, I could stare for a thousand years. See these eyes so red. Oh you've got green eyes, oh you've got blue eyes, oh you've got gray eyes. I'll give you television, I'll give you eyes of blue. I looked in her eyes, they were blue, but nobody home. The blue light was my baby, and the red light was my mind. See these tears so blue. You wouldn't believe what I've been through. It's been so long. And I think it's gonna be a long, long time. It's all over now, Baby Blue.

And there's nothing I can do.

ONE

"Space Oddity" begins with the ten-nine-eight countdown to the rocket blast. As we all learned from *Gravity's Rainbow*, the countdown is something rocket scientists stole from the movies. It originated in a 1929 silent film by Fritz Lang, *Frau im Mond* ("The Woman in the Moon"). Lang added a countdown to the launch scene just for a melodramatic touch. German scientists started counting down to rocket launches at the Raketenflugplatz, and Americans picked it up from them. There's always been an element of showbiz to space travel.

Major Tom is a celebrity—before his spaceship even launches, the papers are calling to ask him to endorse shirts. One of the weird footnotes of the story is that Tom ended up becoming more famous than virtually any real-life astronauts— the only ones who can match him on a celebrity level are Buzz Aldrin, Neil Armstrong, maybe John Glenn or Sally Ride. But that's crucial to the Major Tom fantasy, the assumption that the whole world is watching—if nobody notices him vanish, there's no story. "Space Oddity" is the young Bowie, resentful he's not famous yet, imagining what it's like. For him, the audience *is* outer space. Like an astronaut, a performer is driven by forces he can't control to venture out into the unknown, maybe a hostile place. (Who are those kids out there, anyway? Who can even see them past the stage lights?) Fame felt like that for Bowie. He described it in *Cracked Actor*: "Do you know that feeling you get in a car when somebody's accelerating very fast and you're not driving? And you get that *uuuuh* thing in your chest when you're being forced backwards and you think *uuuuh* and you're not sure whether you like it or not? It's that kind of feeling. That's what success was like."

For Bowie, stepping into the spotlight was stepping through the door—he was desperate for fame, long before he knew precisely what he wanted to do onstage once he arrived. Was he an actor, a mime, a painter? He figured he'd know when he got there. If his moon-landing novelty single had flopped, he would have tried some other hustle a week later. But it hit a nerve with the audience, so he was paired with this guy for life, stuck with a valuable friend. Like the young Tom of "Space Oddity," he had that craving to jump into the darkness, and like the older Tom of "Ashes to Ashes," he found it addictive. He was a passenger in his liftoff to fame, even more than he was the pilot. And you can already hear that in "Space Oddity." He fears that becoming David Bowie will cost him plenty. He fears it will cut him off from human contact (it did) and separate him from his wife (it did) and render him hideous and repulsive to many of his fellow creatures (it most certainly did).

It's a liberating thrill to preen and pose out in space. But the danger is that you can miss out on the passions of a real human earthling. It's like that great scene on *The Wire* where two recovering junkies sit on a park bench late at night, talking about a quote from Kafka. "You can hold back from the suffering of the world. You have free permission to do so, and it is in accordance with your nature. But perhaps this very holding back is the one suffering you could have avoided." Or in other words: my mama said, to get things done, you better not mess with Major Tom.

Too late for second thoughts now. Major Tom is strapped into his space capsule. Engines on. Check ignition. And may God's love be with you. Three. Two. One. Liftoff.

THE QUEEN BITCH
WHO SOLD THE WORLD

1970–1972

And then what? Silence. After "Space Oddity," Bowie seemed to be set up perfectly for his next hit, but unfortunately, the next hit didn't arrive. He felt typecast, complaining, "I just wrote a song about a spaceship and everyone expected me to be some kind of expert." By the time he started recording *The Man Who Sold the World* in the summer of 1970, Bowie was already feeling burned by the business; the title song was the bitter plaint of a washed-up star. He recruited a guitarist named Mick Ronson from a blues band he'd seen up in Hull; producer Tony Visconti played bass. *The Man Who Sold the World* is a great hard rock record, much more bluesy than he'd ever sound again, clearly smitten with Led Zeppelin (and, in "After All," Leonard Cohen). It doesn't sound like any of Bowie's other albums, possibly because Visconti and Ronson did the actual arranging while Bowie spent most of the sessions in bed with his new bride Angie.

On the cover, Bowie poses in a dress (a "man's dress," he explained), daringly unbuttoned. He reclines fetchingly on a sofa with his blond tresses flowing—as he explained, the goal was to look like a Pre-Raphaelite maiden in a Dante Gabriel Rossetti painting, perhaps "Rosa Triplex." It was his first move into brazen gender-bending. The album deserved to be hugely controversial, yet not just for the dress. It mixes up megamasculine blues raunch with Bowie's flamboyantly girlie vocals. On paper, "She Shook Me Cold" might seem like a dubious title, but the song proves Bowie was in a league of his own among male rock stars when it came to sex. He sounds funny and flirtatious and filthy, yet also awestruck by the metaphysical aspects of lust. You can't get much more metaphysical than "We met upon a hill / The night was cool and still / She sucked my dormant will." (A few years later, in his cover of "Let's Spend the Night Together," he changed the line "my tongue's getting tied" to "my tongue's getting tired," which is brilliant in itself.)

It's one of the great kettledrum albums of all time—blame it on Kubrick, but Mick Ronson sure knew how to use kettledrums in a hard-rock context. The eight-minute epic "Width of a Circle" is the furthest out Ronno ever ventured as a guitarist, living up to the artiste's theosophical lyrics. ("Turn around! Go back!") "All the Madmen" was an eerie ballad about being incarcerated in a sanitarium—a fate that had befallen Bowie's elder brother Terry, a schizophrenic. David traveled to the U.S.

for the first time, though visa problems meant he couldn't play any live shows. But he had odd ideas about how to promote a record. He visited KSAN in San Francisco, telling the DJ, "My last LP was, very simply, a collection of reminiscences about my experiences as a shaven-headed transvestite."

Unfortunately, there was no controversy about the album, because hardly anyone knew it existed. His label situation was so chaotic that the album didn't even come out in the UK until six months after its U.S. release, which was a total flop. (The title song remained an obscurity until Kurt Cobain revived it on Nirvana's *MTV Unplugged* special.) And the U.S. version censored the cover photo—it substituted an already-dated-looking Pop Art cartoon of a real-life Victorian mansion. Except by an ugly coincidence, this place happened to be the Cane Hill Asylum, where Bowie's brother Terry lived. Clearly, for Bowie it was time to try something new. Turn around. Go back.

AND THEN ONE DAY DAVID VISITED NEW YORK, WHERE a friend turned him on to the Velvet Underground's "Sweet Jane." The result: *Hunky Dory*, an album of Nico-style café ballads about queen bitches falling in love with pretty things. *Hunky Dory* announced the artist as we came to know him— the dishy, swoony crooner. He's a dream doll on the cover, the essence of a washed-out blond Hollywood starlet—his hair

Harlow gold, his lips pursed for Greta Garbo standoff sighs. As Raymond Chandler's Philip Marlowe would say, he's a blonde to make a bishop kick a hole in a stained-glass window.

On *Hunky Dory* he found his voice, with a lot of help from Mick Ronson's guitar and Rick Wakeman's piano. He wrote songs to act out the future he envisioned, pretending he was already a dotty showbiz grande dame, the over-the-hill actress Lou Reed serenaded in "New Age." "Queen Bitch" pays tribute to the Velvets while giving David a chance to look swishy in his bipperty-bopperty hat. He gossips about Andy Warhol and Bob Dylan. "Life on Mars?" began as an attempt to cop the French chanson "Comme d'Habitude" and write English words to it; Paul Anka beat him to it with "My Way," which became Frank Sinatra's signature song. On the album sleeve Bowie inscribed "Life on Mars?" as "inspired by Frankie." (Aretha Franklin recorded "My Way," a 1970 outtake that didn't get released until years later. I love it because it's the closest we'll ever get to my fantasy of Aretha singing "Life on Mars?")

Bowie was angling himself as the first seventies rock star— the one who called time on the sixties and announced it was all over. Time for bigger dreams and gaudier colors. He billed himself as "the Actor" on the back cover, to make sure nobody mistook him for one of those sincere bloody hippie types. The future race was coming to take over the world—the pretty things, driving their mamas and papas insane—and not a moment too soon. When Bowie curls his lip around the line "All the nightmares came today," you can hear him thinking "and what took you so long?"

Bowie arrived late for the sixties party, so he missed the idealistic hippie days and had to settle for being the quintessential seventies rock star along with Neil Young. It's funny how much those two have in common, despite their opposite fashion sense. Both arrived as solo artists just as the sixties were imploding, a little too late to be Bob Dylan, and they never got over it. Both built their massive seventies mystique around abrupt stylistic shifts. Both fluked into a Number 1 hit ("Fame" and "Heart of Gold"), but both responded to this success by refusing to repeat it, much to the despair of their record companies. Both wrote gorgeous sci-fi ballads blatantly inspired by *2001*—"Space Oddity" and "After the Gold Rush." Both did classic songs about imperialism that name-checked Marlon Brando—"China Girl" and "Pocahontas." Both were prodigiously prolific even when they were trying to eat Peru through their nostrils. They were mutual fans, though they floundered when they tried to copy each other (*Trans* and *Tin Machine*). Both sang their fears of losing their youth when they were still basically kids; both aged mysteriously well. Neither ever did anything remotely sane.

But there's a key difference: Bowie liked working with smart people, whereas Young always liked working with . . .

well, let's go ahead and call them "not quite as smart as Neil Young" people. Young made his most famous music with two backing groups—the awesomely inept Crazy Horse and the expensively addled CSN—whose collective IQ barely leaves room temperature. He must know they're not going to challenge him with ideas of their own, so he knows how to use them— brilliantly in the first case, lucratively in the second. But Bowie never made any of his memorable music that way—he always preferred collaborating with (and stealing from) artists who knew tricks he didn't know, well educated in musical worlds where he was just a visitor. Just look at the guitarists he worked with: Carlos Alomar from James Brown's band vs. Robert Fripp from King Crimson. Stevie Ray Vaughan from Texas vs. Mick Ronson from Hull. Adrian Belew from Kentucky vs. Earl Slick from Brooklyn. Nile Rodgers. Peter Frampton. Ricky Gardiner, who played all that fantastic fuzz guitar on *Low* (and who made the mistake of demanding a raise, which is why he dropped out of the story so fast).

Together, Young and Bowie laid claim to a jilted generation left high and dry by the dashed hippie dreams. "The sixties are definitely not with us anymore," Neil said in 1973. "The change into the music of the seventies is starting to come with people like David Bowie and Lou Reed. . . . Homosexualism and heavy dope use and everything is a way of life to a lotta people—and they don't expect to live any more than thirty years, and they don't care. And they don't care. They're in the seventies. What I'm tryin' to say is these people like Lou Reed and David Booie or Bowie, however you pronounce it, those folks—I think they got somethin' there, heh heh. Take a walk on the wild side!"

On May 28, 1971, Bowie was at home listening to a Neil Young record when he got a phone call from the hospital. His wife (you remember her, Angie) had just given birth. He celebrated by writing a song called "Kooks," which he debuted live a few days later on John Peel's radio program. (The song has a Dionne Warwick/Burt Bacharach flavor, especially the trumpet solo—which means the Neil song he had on the brain was probably "Till The Morning Comes.") He was singing to his own son Zowie, but he may as well have been singing about the seventies kids who would soon cling to him, though not necessarily as a paternal figure. The parents and the kid in this song are both on the same level—kooks, hung up on romancing, despised by the bullies and the cads of the straight society. They're the pretty things, the Homo Superior of the future.

You can see that in a clip Bowie taped for the BBC program *The Old Grey Whistle Test*. He sits down at the piano to sing "Oh! You Pretty Things" straddling the bench in a jumpsuit with the front buttons undone. He already seems otherworldly, staring into the camera with his disarming off-color eyes. But nobody knew yet how far out he was planning to get. The future was now. Bowie was that future.

THE STARMAN

1972

Ziggy Stardust finally made Bowie the massive rock and roll scandal he had always desperately wanted to be. "Five Years" sets the scene, as those apocalyptic drums fade in: acoustic guitar, piano, strings, the end of the world. Bowie walks through a city in chaos. He sees people wandering the streets in shock and fury, kissing and fighting and weeping and breaking every social taboo. Panic on the streets of London. He falls in love with every last one of them. A crowd begins to sing. The song ends with these strangers standing in the rain together, chanting "Five years! That's all we've got!" as the city burns and quakes around them. A few hours ago, they were all home watching the news on TV, bored out of their heads. Isn't this more exciting?

The plot of *Ziggy Stardust* never really made any sense, as Bowie freely conceded. But the concept of the album is right there in "Five Years," in that mood of urgency—a challenge to seize life like right now is all you've got. In *The Man Who Fell to Earth*, one of the film clips flashing through the alien's brain is Gary Cooper in Billy Wilder's *Love in the Afternoon*, telling the young lovestruck Audrey Hepburn, "I think people should always behave as though they were between planes"—a line that could just as easily have come from Ziggy. It's a song about how you get a reminder of mortality and it makes you take stock of the people littered around the warehouse of your brain and makes you love them a little more savagely than you used to, which means (among other things) devouring them for fantasy material, with all the innocent bystanders (and milk shake drinkers) who unwillingly (and unknowingly) become the stars of the movie in your head and the song ringing in your ears. "It was cold and it rained so I felt like an actor"—what a one-line manifesto of Bowieism. He doesn't fantasize about being the hero or the gangster or the showgirl, just the actor inhabiting the role.

"Five Years" shows off Bowie's unerring instinct for opening songs—he must hold some kind of record when it comes to putting the album's mission statement up front. ("Young Americans," "Changes," "Station to Station," "Watch That Man," "Speed of Life," "Sunday," "Modern Love"—what a run.) More than one kid I knew grew up thinking the "fiiiive yeeeears!" chant was "fuck yes." The hook "My brain hurts a lot" might evoke *Monty Python*—you could definitely argue there's Python humor in Bowie's music by this point—but the "Gumby Brain Specialist" sketch didn't air until November 1972, so this seems like a clear case of great minds (with hurting brains) thinking alike. The song also feels like a sly parody of John Lennon's "Imagine"—yes, Bowie imagines all the people living for today, except it doesn't mean peace and love, it means crazed pedestrians roaming the streets attacking mobs of children while cop-on-priest sex inspires incidents of public regurgitation.

After "Five Years," Bowie could have spent the rest of the album making gnome jokes and he still would have scored a hit. But he wanted the entire LP to be a sensation. When he put the final running order together with producer Ken Scott, there was a song on side 1 that didn't quite make the grade: a cover of Chuck Berry's "Round and Round." It fit the concept—the kind of oldie the Spiders from Mars would have covered—but redundant, given that side 2 was already full of Chuck Berry rips. Side 1 needed something different, something bigger and loftier. An anthem. Bowie dutifully flitted off and rushed out one more tune to squeeze onto the album at the last minute. He called it "Starman."

"Starman" turned into the fabled *Top of the Pops* performance of July 6, 1972—the moment where Bowie truly conquered Britannia. He strums a blue acoustic guitar, with tangerine hair, a rainbow catsuit, and astronaut boots, casually draping an arm around Mick Ronson. In just four minutes, he went from a plodding folkie to England's most infamous rock sensation. Every future legend in the British Isles was tuned in. Morrissey was watching. So was Johnny Marr. Siouxsie was watching. Robert Smith was watching. Duran Duran were watching. So were Echo and the Bunnymen. Dave Gahan. Jarvis Cocker. Noel Gallagher. U2. Bauhaus. Jesus, Mary, and their Chain. Bloody everybody. It's no coincidence that there was a boom of English rock stars born between 1958 and 1963—these were the kids stuck at home on a Thursday night in 1972, watching an otherwise depressing hour of *Top of the Pops*. As Bono told *Rolling Stone* in 2010, "The first time I saw him was singing 'Starman' on television. It was like a creature falling from the sky. Americans put a man on the moon. We had our own British guy from space—with an Irish mother."

It's easy for a benighted American to marvel at how so many Brits got hit by the thunderbolt that evening; it was Duran Duran's Nick Rhodes and John Taylor who schooled me to the blindingly obvious fact that the UK had scarcely any TV channels, three on a good night, and *everybody* watched *Top of the Pops* no matter how devoid of enthusiasm or low their expectations. Watching the clip today, in our jaded video-saturated world, it's still simple to see why Bowie spilled a nation's beans on toast. The most shocking detail isn't his hair, it's his beatific smile—he makes Mick Jagger look like somebody's neurotic papa, waggling his finger at the camera for that "you-hoo-hoo." He *loves* being this guy. Everybody's welcome here: the man with the blue guitar, his Spiders, the bassist with the bleached muttonchops, the befuddled-looking dancing boy in the sweater vest, the Asian fangirl in the pink prom dress, the elderly lady with the white Bea Arthur beehive getting down in the corner. All are accepted. It's true that Bowie wasn't up against heavyweights—the rest of the show included Gary Glitter, Sweet, and the Partridge Family—but he faced the best pop had to offer in 1972 and turned them all into background scenery.

Even more than *Hunky Dory*, Ziggy served notice and called time on the sixties and celebrated a tawdry new school of seventies rock pretensions. He was already mocking the "brothers back at home with their Beatles and their Stones" in 1972, barely two years after the Beatles split—and not only did the Stones still exist, they'd just dropped their best album. Bowie was drawing his generational lines, making a joke out of it, especially since you only had to listen to the music to know that it was written by a brother who took his Beatles and Stones very personally indeed. But Bowie was eager to dance on the grave of the sixties and move on.

"Ziggy Stardust" is an empathetic song that only a true prima donna could have written about himself in the third person, taking stock of all the damage he was leaving behind in his wake for the increasingly large number of people who had to clean up after him and sweep the glitter off the floor. Just as "Starman" didn't reveal much about the starman, "Ziggy Stardust" isn't really about Ziggy at all. It's a song about the other guys in the band—from their first-person-plural perspective, figuring out this strange charismatic creature who rocketed through their drab lives and left them with pain to heal from and anger to forgive. They don't know how Ziggy ever felt about them—he was too wrapped up in making love with his ego—just that they're still confused by this monster of vanity and beauty and cruelty. It has the tone of the Acts of the Apostles—the starman has ascended and left his decidedly unheroic followers to fumble on with work to do despite the fact that they don't really know or like each other much or have anything in common aside from this pushy little leper messiah who showed up and bossed them around for a few years. The song wouldn't exist if Ziggy were still alive—they'd still just be bitching about their stuck-up lead singer. But now that he's gone, all they can do is write a bittersweet melody in his honor—much as Pink Floyd would do years later, mourning Syd Barrett with "Wish You Were Here."

Ziggy was a requiem: Bowie came to bury the sixties, not praise them. He hit the road and toured like a madman, spreading the glitter gospel in a rock scene full of interchangeable flannel-and-denim sincerity pimps. English kids responded with a fervor that must have stunned even him—they started dressing up, acting out, walking the Ziggy walk. As the tour kept rolling, so did the sex and drugs, the tabloid headlines and audience screams, which just encouraged his messianic fantasies to get loopier. One night in Newcastle, when the bouncers pushed the kids around a little too much for his liking, he announced, "There are two stars in rock and roll—me and the audience. And if those stewards don't stop . . . the stars are going to make this place into a matchbox." He and Mick Ronson added a little special something to the show; when Ronno played a solo, Bowie dropped to his knees and simulated oral sex on his guitar. For some reason, this made an impression on people. He was dressing the part full-time, offstage and on. He glammed up the Spiders, too, which was rough on three down-to-earth lads from Hull. "I like to keep my group well dressed, not like some other people I could mention," he declared. "I'm out to bloody well entertain, not just get up onstage and knock out a few songs."

By the time the tour reached London on July 3, 1973, for one big climax at the Hammersmith Odeon, Ziggy's audience was an even more out-of-control rock and roll beast than he was. Documentary director D. A. Pennebaker was on hand to film the final performance and recalled, "It was so different, more vibrant than anything in the States. I was astonished at how he had the whole goddamn audience singing backup for him. I thought: 'How'd he arrrange that? Did he have instructional Saturdays where everybody came and rehearsed? What was this?'"

What nobody could have predicted was that Bowie was already planning to bury Ziggy. Onstage in London, he surprised everyone—including the long-suffering boys in his band—with the announcement, "Not only is this the last show of the tour, it's the last show that we'll ever do. Thank you." The crowd wailed, *"Noooo!"* It was a theatrical twist worthy of a master, and the "Bowie Quits" headlines that followed proved it was a publicity coup. The star who killed the sixties was already killing the seventies. Bowie wasn't retiring, of course, just slaying his alter ego with a *wham bam, thank you ma'am*. It was the first time he'd broken his audience's heart—but hardly the last. He had other roles to play and other hearts to break.

THE NIGHT
ZIGGY MET AMERICA

1972

It makes sense that Ziggy had to come to California to become a true star. The Pacific Ocean is the hole where the moon used to be—millions of years ago, the moon launched itself into orbit around the earth, floating in a most peculiar way, leaving a cavity that became the ocean. Bowie had to go there—only he could make it whole again.

And Bowie needed America. Until he made it there, he hadn't made it on his own terms—he needed a stage that grand, or else his whole concept would have been a flop. The kind of stardom Bowie was playing with needed American girls to scream over it, otherwise it was just an art project. He needed America the way a stripper needs a pole, the way a queen needs a throne. "One is not duchess a hundred yards from a carriage," as Wallace Stevens said, and the kind of duchess Bowie aspired to be needed a carriage as vast and tacky as America.

It really clicked when he came to Santa Monica on October 20, 1972, a show recorded for radio broadcast and prized by fans as a bootleg years before it ever got legally released. This was his first real American tour, with the Spiders from Mars, just after *Ziggy Stardust* came out here. And until he got to Southern California, the tour was a washout, playing to mostly empty houses in the Midwest. Some shows were canceled for low ticket sales. He knocked them dead in Cleveland, the first U.S. city hip to Bowie, but NYC dismissed him as a hype. "We had our downs," he says diplomatically in the book *Moonage Daydream*. "St. Louis was not a Ziggy town." In Kansas City, hardly anyone showed up, so he invited the crowd up to sit on the edge of the stage, until he tumbled off drunk. But the West Coast is where America met Bowie and fell in love. That night in Santa Monica, he finally became the special man.

Bizarrely, which is how many sentences about Bowie begin, you can hear it happen when you listen to the Santa Monica bootleg: the star and the audience get louder and chattier as the show goes on, like a blind date gone horribly right. Halfway through the show, after "Five Years," the girls start to shriek "DAVID!" Until tonight, they probably had no idea who he was. They were just looking for a place to party. A couple of hours ago, they thought Deep Purple was the shit. Now they're Those Bowie Girls.

It's a pivotal chapter in the long-running and always-fascinating romance between English rock stars and California girls. So much of the world's favorite music comes out of that bond. For English rock boys, the goal was always to inspire crush juice in the lips and loins of California girls. Those were the fans they dreamed about. For any band worth its salt out of sleepy London town, the motivation to write great songs was to stir the amatory nectars of the sun-kissed vestals of the West Coast, to attract those girls and reward them for their devotion. And the more fiercely the California handmaidens loved them, the better the bands got—a feedback loop that improved all our lives. Ever since the Beatles wrote "Drive My Car" ("to me it was L.A. chicks," Paul said) that bond held strong, and nobody wooed those girls like Bowie. At the Santa Monica show, he's face-to-face with those girls—he sings, they scream, he sings louder, they scream louder.

At first, he's timid, realizing they're hearing the tunes for the first time. But as the show goes on, he starts to soar on the crowd energy, saying things like "You're terrific." He might also be soaring on something else, judging from the way he improvises poetry like, "I asked for lobster tail and they brought me palm tree." He's doing all these songs they couldn't possibly know, some that haven't been released yet ("The Jean Genie") and obscure covers (Lou Reed, Jacques Brel). He's doing songs from *Hunky Dory*, no kind of hit in America, and *Ziggy Stardust*, which he'd just released; "Space Oddity" is the only tune that gets a "hey, we know this one" clap at the intro. For the rocket launch, Bowie mimics the roar of the engines with his mouth, a sound that's both silly and touching. The Spiders from Mars play a little faster than they need to—everyone's swept up in the excitement. When they rip into "Hang On to Yourself," they sound like the Sex Pistols. (Famously, the Pistols stole their microphones and PA system from Bowie after his 1973 show in London.) When Mick Ronson and Bowie join voices at the climax of "Five Years," they're nowhere near the same key, but too blissed out to notice, which was part of the message.

These are the kids Zeppelin wrote "Going to California" about, but Bowie's a lot less coy about his affection for them. He declares that they're much hipper than their older brothers and sisters, that the corrupt adult world won't crush them, that their golden years are just beginning. And they decide they like what they hear. Of course, there's a lot of heartbreak ahead for Bowie and his new audience—drugs, despair, *Soul Train*. L.A. would nearly destroy Bowie a few years later. But tonight, he's a star because he makes them feel like stars. The California kids are face-to-face with something commensurate to their capacity for wonder. For once, they're not alone. And neither is he.

THE FIRST HIT HE WROTE IN AMERICA WAS "THE JEAN Genie," inspired by a true American muse. He wrote it as a little bump and grind for Cyrinda Foxe, the ultimate New York Bowie girl of the early seventies—as Bowie put it, "a consort of the Marilyn brand." The platinum-blond Miss Foxe was later married to both Steven Tyler and David Johansen, but she's beloved by Bowie fans as the girl who taught him how to shop for shoes, tutoring him in the art of wearing "palm-tree'd fuck-me pumps."

As Bowie recalled, with an Englishman's customary disregard for dangling modifiers: "Starting out as a lightweight riff thing I had written one evening in NYC for Cyrinda's enjoyment, I developed the lyric to the otherwise wordless pumper and it ultimately turned into a bit of a smorgasbord of imagined Americana. Its central character was based on an Iggy-type persona and the setting was inspired by Max's Kansas City." (No other NYC locale inspired English rock boys like this one—Marc Bolan's "Baby Boomerang," John Lennon's "New York City," Mick Jagger's "Do You Think I Really Care?") As a Warhol protégée, Foxe knew this scene from the inside. As Bowie recalled fondly, "Although she had been exposed to the most caustic and world-weary set of queens ever unleashed, she retained innocence and had a light but effective sense of humor." That's why I love "The Jean Genie"—Genet or no Genet, it always feels like Cyrinda's song. In a way, she was as crucial as Iggy or Lou to Bowie's sense of sexy American trash—although he enjoyed pumping her for gossip about hanging with Warhol and Duchamp. He also liked to wear her earrings onstage.

They filmed a video together for "The Jean Genie" in California, directed by Mick Rock. Nothing fancy: Bowie and Cyrinda frolic on the streets of San Francisco, in front of the Mars Hotel, shaking what mama gave them in matching James Dean–style leather jackets. You can see how cocky Bowie is: out on the West Coast, in the open air, wearing the highest heels and dancing with the foxiest fox, worlds away from the dim London road he roamed in "Five Years." He and America are giving each other what they crave. He takes a look around and he lets himself go.

ALADDIN SANE

1973

Rest in peace, Ziggy Stardust—long live Aladdin Sane. Just a year after seducing the world with the saga of Ziggy, Bowie killed him off to invent a new glam character—a much darker one, with a new haircut and a lightning bolt painted over his face. "There was a point in '73 where I knew it was all over," Bowie explained. "I didn't want to be trapped in this Ziggy character all my life. And I guess what I was doing on *Aladdin Sane*, I was trying to move into the next area—but using a rather pale imitation of Ziggy as a secondary device. In my mind it was *Ziggy Goes to Washington*: Ziggy under the influence of America."

A sinister influence, to be sure. *Aladdin Sane* is a harder, nastier, kinkier story than *Ziggy Stardust*, written on the road and immersed in the sleaze of American culture. Each song on the sleeve is listed with the place that inspired it—"Watch That Man" in New York, "Drive-In Saturday" on the train from Seattle to Phoenix, "Lady Grinning Soul" back in London. But everywhere he goes, he sees cheap sex and cheaper drugs. *Alad-*

din Sane was Bowie's response to the USA—now that he'd made it there, he wasn't so sure he liked it. "Cracked Actor" sets the tone—instead of a starry-eyed thespian, this actor is a washed-up Hollywood star, picking up a young junkie hooker on the corner of Sunset and Vine. This isn't the theater kid from *Ziggy Stardust* who sang "It was cold and it rained so I felt like an actor"— this is a corrupt has-been who watches his old movies on TV while begging his hired groupie to "suck, baby, suck." The actor is fifty—nearly twice Bowie's age at the time. Just a couple of years after Bowie fantasized his way to stardom, he was already picturing himself wilted and faded somewhere in Hollywood.

David and Angie were rock's royal couple, proudly flaunting the most open of marriages. He was still by far the world's most high-profile out gay or bi man, though he was accused of using it as a gimmick. "It's true, I am bisexual," he told Cameron Crowe. "But I can't deny I've used the fact very well. I suppose it's the best thing that has ever happened to me. Fun, too." Why? "Well, for one thing, girls are always presuming that I've kept my heterosexual virginity for some reason. So I've had all these girls to try to get me over to the other side again. 'C'mon David, it isn't all that bad. I'll show you.' Or better yet, 'We'll show you.' I always play dumb."

Bowie wrote the songs amid the frenzy of touring, with the working title *Love Aladdin Vein*. (In that same crazed year, he produced Lou Reed's *Transformer* and mixed the Stooges' *Raw Power*.) The music expanded as avant-jazz pianist Mike Garson joined the Spiders from Mars. A Scientologist, he spent the tour trying to convert the boys in the band, adding to the general chaos. It all proved Bowie's theory that if he could get famous, something must be wrong. "People like Lou and I are probably predicting the end of an era," he proclaimed. "Any society that allows people like Lou and me to become rampant is pretty well lost. We're both pretty mixed-up, paranoid people—absolute walking messes. If we're the spearhead of anything, we're not necessarily the spearhead of anything good."

Compared to Aladdin, the Bowie of *Ziggy Stardust* sounds downright innocent and idealistic—a hippie, really. A year ago, he was pleading, "Don't fake it baby / Lay the real thing on me." Now in "Cracked Actor," he's telling that hooker "Show me you're real"—or is it "Show me your reel," the classic casting-couch come-on? Who knows—the hooker's probably an aspiring movie star as well. No doubt he or she hopes to move into a mansion just like this one, after the current resident finishes boozing his way to skid row. Either way, it's a nasty affair. The young American rock and roll fellatio machine goes to work, while the cracked actor dreams about his Hollywood highs of yesteryear. The real thing ain't as real as it used to be.

AROUND THIS TIME BOWIE ALSO DID *THE 1980 FLOOR Show*, his infamous American TV bash for *The Midnight Special*, hosted by Wolfman Jack. Bowie outdid himself spectacle-wise, with costumes designed by Freddie Buretti. He plays "The Jean Genie" wearing a black-mesh spiderweb shirt with a pair of hands clutching his chest—glittering gold lamé hands, long black fingernails—to give the impression David's getting groped from behind while singing. A third hand, reaching between his legs to fondle his crotch, was removed at the insistence of the censors, although without the hand the outfit looks even more obscene, leaving him daringly bare in the nether regions.

The showstopper: Bowie dons a red vinyl corset with black ostrich-feather wings to sing Sonny & Cher's "I Got You Babe" as a duet with Marianne Faithfull, who's dressed as a nun in full habit. Well, not quite full—just the front half. As Bowie recalled, "Because of her convent background, I felt Marianne would carry the moment superbly as a nun, albeit without a back panel to her habit, revealing her splendid arse." Alas, U.S. TV wasn't ready to permit a glimpse of Sister Faithfull's naked dorsal altar from behind. But she sings in her funniest (and most out-of-tune) Lotte Lenya/Marlene Dietrich monotone, gazing up at Bowie with rapt devotion. Poor Wolfman Jack looks horrified—when he announces that the next episode will be a B. B. King special, he asks the studio audience, "You guys dig blues, right?" It's his way of promising shocked American viewers it'll be safe to come back next week for, you know, *real* music.

DESPITE ITS DEBAUCHED TONE, *ALADDIN* WAS AN even bigger hit than *Ziggy*. Bowie had finally topped his old glam rival Marc Bolan, the Warlock of Love. T. Rex had made two enduring classics in a rush—*Electric Warrior* and *The Slider*—but Bolan sadly lost his touch overnight and crashed into an alcoholic haze. Before long, he was doing his own Ziggy rip-off, *Zinc Alloy and the Riders of Tomorrow*. Yet he still wasn't impressed by the mime with the crap shoes. He told *Creem* in 1973 Bowie didn't have star power. "He just doesn't have that sort of quality," the Warlock said. "I do. I always have. Rod Stewart has it in his own mad way. Elton John has it. Mick Jagger has that quality. Michael Jackson has that quality. David Bowie doesn't, I'm sorry to say." (Ten years before *Thriller*—now that's a prophet talking.) Gracious in victory, Bowie eventually renewed their friendship—one day in 1977, after a tipsy lunch, they roamed down the King's Road together singing out loud. They attempted to annoy a busful of schoolchildren by jumping up and down yelling, "I'm David Bowie!" "I'm Marc Bolan!" The kids were not impressed. When Bolan attempted a comeback with a TV variety show, Bowie joined him for a brief jam session, until Bolan tumbled off the stage and they both burst into laughter. Sadly, it was the final reconciliation for the glam gods: Bolan was killed in a car wreck less than two weeks later.

Bowie was pumping out songs so fast in the early seventies,

he gave away hits like candy. When he heard Mott the Hoople were splitting up out of commercial frustration, he wrote "All the Young Dudes" for them, just to keep the band together. When he played it for them on his guitar, they were afraid to ask why he'd taken leave of his senses so completely as to hand them a song this great. It became the definitive glam hymn, an ode to tarted-up boys and girls looting and pillaging and making out in the streets, ending with a strange monologue where lead singer Ian Hunter singles out a young dude in the audience ("you there, in the glasses—I want you") and has him dragged up front for some kind of depraved public sex ritual. (Hunter later said he simply imagined pouring beer on a heckler's head. Sure.) He offered Mott another sure thing, "Drive-In Saturday," a doo-wop ballad set in a future nuclear apocalypse where humans have forgotten how sex works, and have to learn the basics by watching old Mick Jagger footage. But they turned it down. "I was so angry, I shaved my cyebrows off. I kid you not."

While waiting for his brows to grow back in, Bowie consoled himself with his own version of "Drive-In Saturday," which became a Number 3 UK hit. He released *Aladdin Sane* in April 1973, three months before he killed Ziggy Stardust onstage in London. As far as the industry was concerned, Bowie had just arrived. But with *Aladdin Sane*, he was already restless for parts unknown.

THE CRACKED ACTOR

1974

Bowie starred in the scariest documentary ever to catch a rock star in the midst of the madness—the BBC's *Cracked Actor*, directed by Alan Yentob, chasing Bowie on tour in the USA. The most indelible scene: Bowie in the back of his limo, riding through the desert, pale and emaciated under his hat, gulping from a carton of milk. "There's a fly floating around in my milk," Bowie says. "That's kind of how I felt [in America]—a foreign body and I couldn't help but soak it up. . . . It filled the vast expanse of my imagination. It just supplied a need in me, America. It became a mythland for me."

Bowie looks through the window at the Movieland Wax Museum and giggles. "A bleeding wax museum in the desert? Think it'd melt, wouldn't you?" But Bowie himself is a wax museum, looking frail and vulnerable everywhere he goes except onstage. Rolling through L.A. late at night, all dolled up in the back of his limo, he flinches in panic at the sound of a police siren ("Hope we're not stopped?"), and emits the world's loud-est sniffle—as if he's trying to snort any stray speck of powder that might still be lodged in his nostrils. His hair piled high, the neon lights reflected on his makeup, he looks uncannily like Rue McClanahan playing Blanche on *The Golden Girls*.

It looks like the myths are devouring him faster than the drugs, especially when he does "Sweet Thing" from *Diamond Dogs*, his concept job about Orwellian peoploids. But the af-fection between the star and his fans is real, which gives the movie its strange warmth. His American fans know the BBC camera crew is snickering at them when they go off about lov-ing Bowie, but they do not care. A roomful of longhair boys explain why Ziggy is an allegory about the death of Jimi Hen-drix. A dude in a top hat says, "I never get bored because I can always change." A glitter chick gushes, "I'm just a space cadet—he's the commander!"

Bowie warms up when he talks about the kids—they're the only human beings in his world who stir his emotions in any way. He refuses to take credit for their glam style—they're the creative artists. "They're finding out things maybe nothing to do with me, but the idea of finding another character within themselves," Bowie says. "I mean, if I've been at all responsi-ble for people finding more characters in themselves than they originally thought they had, then I'm pleased, because that's something I feel very strongly about. That one isn't totally what one has been conditioned to think one is. That there are many facets of the personality that many of us have trouble finding." There's a grim trace of a smile on his lips. "And some of us do find too quickly."

Most of the fans in *Cracked Actor* look like ordinary midwestern stoners in jeans, probably the same crowd that comes to any rock show in town. But Bowie brings something out of them. One of my heroes is the burnout guy with the feathered mullet, the one who looks like Fred Armisen playing Tom Petty, sprawled out on the sidewalk outside the arena. "He's from his own universe," the kid raves. "The Bowie universe!" The BBC interviewer asks, "Have *you* been to the Bowie universe?" The fan tries to explain, as if he's talking to an idiot. "He's the center. I was drawn to it." So how did he discover the Bowie universe? He shrugs. "I'm from Phoenix, and . . . I just . . . came."

That was the original Bowie crowd. He saw beauty in those kids. And he made them see beauty in themselves.

THE MOST CHILLING MOMENT ON *DIAMOND DOGS* IS the song he left off—the "Candidate" demo that went unheard by even the most devoted Bowie-ologists until it came out as a bonus track on the 1990 Rykodisc reissue. Anybody else could have built a legend on a song this great. Bowie left it in the vault—it isn't even one of his hundred most famous tunes. But it's one of my favorites, and it's one where he perfected a few tricks that would carry him through the decade.

"Candidate (Demo)" shouldn't be confused with the "Candidate" midsection of the "Sweet Thing" triptych—the songs have nothing in common except a line of the lyrics. It's a shame "Candidate (Demo)" (also labeled as "Alternative Candidate" on later packages) doesn't have a real title of its own, because it's been overshadowed—yet it would have been the prettiest and nastiest piece of work on *Diamond Dogs*. No studio special effects—just insistent guitar and piano, as Bowie takes a Lou Reed–like slow-motion strut through the city, preening and parading. He introduces himself as the rock star you pass every day on the street and don't notice: "I make it a thing when I gazelle onstage to believe in myself / I make it a thing to glance in windowpanes and look pleased with myself."

He pretends he's walking home, but he's really just flitting from shop window to shop window so he can admire his reflection. The whole city is his glittering mirror—or yours, if you're willing to seize it that way. Walking through the streets makes you a candidate—the urban pedestrian as rock star, the flaneur as auteur. Every sidewalk is your stage. If you're not sure you have the ego to pull it off, just follow him—you can both pretend you're walking home. He'll use you as a decoy when he shoplifts a new pair of jeans. (And before you know it, he's vanished with your money. You should have known better than to trust him.) As always when rock stars sing about mirrors, there's the suspicion there's a drug or two involved. There's also a whiff of sex ("Inside every teenage girl is a fountain," oh really) and an ominous hint of fascist tyranny on the way. Well, not even a hint—this candidate announces "I'm the Führerling," which isn't a real German word but can't mean anything good. The lyrics are mere cutups, or maybe even placeholders he didn't get around to finishing, but the vocals are so seductive that the sinister mood builds throughout the song.

"Candidate (Demo)" sounds like the template for Iggy's "The Passenger" and "Nightclubbing," as well as Bowie's own 1980 hit "Fashion." It's the essential Bowie night-stalking psycho-fop march. "Candidate (Demo)" could only have been written in a blaze of rampant egomania—an ode to the pleasures of solipsism, starring Bowie as a one-man goon squad who's coming to town. Pure uncut "I could be king," without a drop of "you could be queen." The song makes you feel the intense pleasure of being a world-class poseur on Bowie's level— damn, what a blast it would be to spend thirty seconds of your life that consumed by your own glamour. And what torture it would be to descend from that high back into the real world. When you're high, you never ever wanna come down.

YOUNG AMERICANS

1975

My favorite David Bowie song is either "Young Americans" or "Station to Station," and it's maddening to keep going back and forth on this over the years. But maybe I keep changing my mind because it's fun to change your mind about things. That's one of the things David Bowie came to show us—we go to music to hear ourselves change.

When I first heard "Young Americans" (a Sunday night around dusk, the stereo in my grandmother's living room, WCOZ, on headphones), I was a very young American indeed. I was thirteen, and all I wanted was to be as old and wise as the twenty-year-olds in the third verse—wow, these kids had *lived*. I couldn't wait to be them—so fraught with philosophical questions, so caught up in cross-country adventures, so worldly and tragic and knowing. I fell in love with the song, permanently, hopelessly, by the time the chorus kicked in: "All night, she wants the young American." I wanted to be that girl (the one who does the wanting) and I also wanted to be the young American she wanted. I could not *wait* to grow up and become one of these young Americans.

When I was seventeen, it was a grittier song, with jokes I didn't catch before. I remember hearing it on the debate-team bus, on the way back after a tournament, and noticing "it took him minutes, it took her nowhere"—oh wait, *that's* what it means. By the time I was married with bills to pay, that haunting question—"We've lived for just these twenty years, do we have to die for the fifty more?"—felt totally different. When I play the song now, I hear things in Bowie's voice I had no way of recognizing when I was thirteen or seventeen or twenty-five. I hear crags in his voice. I hear warmth and self-mockery and fear. I hear that he's a little ashamed of himself for presuming to belt like Aretha, but I also hear that he drops to his knees and belts anyway. Some nights, the guy who sings "Young Americans" still sounds older and wiser than I am. Other times, but not as often, he's just a kid. I have not yet reached the point where I hear the song and think "This guy isn't alive right now," but that will happen. The Bowie in this song is always mutating, and he makes me hear the ways I'm mutating too.

"Young Americans" is one of those songs that has trailed me around forever, so I hear all my changes in it. To me, it's my favorite story Bowie ever had to tell, not so much in the lyrics as the way he sings it—huffing, croaking, pleading, whimpering. The fact that huge chunks of the lyrics are utterly incomprehensible is a crucial part of the story he's telling. "You ain't a pervert, you ain't a whore, sir, a man's gotta carry on and maybe drive a Chrysler, blacks got their Stanford, whites got their *Soul Train*"—something like that, more or less? Who knows? I've never seen a transcription that got anywhere close, and given Bowie's state of mind in 1975, his guess wasn't any better than yours. He loved to keep playing with the words over the years, just like Dylan keeps playing with "Tangled Up in Blue" (his own "Young Americans"). I love how he twisted his question near the end of the song: "Is there a woman who can say any more? Is there a man I can sock on the jaw?"

But my favorite part—my favorite moment in any Bowie song—comes at the end, when the Dame goes into that dizzy heavy-breathing incantation. He glances at the clock, notices he's closing in on the five-minute mark, feels exhausted from everything he's confessed already, but realizes his song's almost over and he hasn't really gotten to the point yet. So he throws up his hands and just *tells* it: "I want what you want. I want what you want. You want them, I want you, you want I, I want you want. I want what you want, but you want what they want you, you want I, I want you. And all I want is the young American."

Well, that clears everything up. It's taken Bowie the entire song to arrive here, but just by wanting the young American, he gets to feel like a real live human for a moment. I love every second of the song but especially that final minute. It's tragic when the DJ tries to shave 15 or 20 seconds off the song by fading out early—every karaoke version I've ever seen fades way too fast. He needs us to understand that he's David Bowie and he hopes we all get what our hearts desire and oh yes, he would also very much like to have sex with each and every one of us tonight. He wants to be a young American, he wants to do a young American, but most of all he wants to participate in our *want* somehow.

BOWIE WAS CHANGING FAST WHEN HE MADE THIS record. After conquering America and turning into the decadent glam god of *Diamond Dogs*, he needed a new beat—he needed to jolt himself into feeling something. So he went to Philly to make a soul record, and this song came together the first night of the sessions. Bowie sounds old and vampirish, though he was only twenty-seven (just as Neil Young was only twenty-six when he sang "and I'm gettin' old" in his lone Number 1 hit). It's a song of affection for the kids in his audience, and the moms and dads they're leaving behind.

"It's about a newlywed couple who don't know if they really like each other," Bowie explained at the time. To Bowie, the kids in this song are as noble as the lovers under the Berlin

Wall in "'Heroes.'" These kids are the real thing—they fall in love, they get their hearts broken, they beg on the bathroom floor. Bowie looks kindly at their sincere but inept sexual fumbling. He sees them feeling real emotions and weeping hot tears he's too dead inside to share, and he grieves for that. But their warmth makes him feel a little toastier, and by the end of the song he actually finds himself suffering through a feeling or two himself. These kids make him feel a little more real. So does the bored housewife in the second verse—Bowie makes her sound like a Mrs. Robinson, the mom of one of these kids, worrying it's all passed her by. Until she looks out her window and sees that slinky vagabond in her driveway, humping her new car. She wants that young American. Hey, maybe it's not too late. In my heart, at least, she and the vagabond end up in the back of the Mustang, parked under the same bridge as the kids in the first verse.

Bowie sings about them with so much compassion and generosity, not to mention lechery. He roots for them to stand by each other with love, togetherness, and devotion, even though he isn't capable of it himself. He knows he can never be as pure of heart, as uncorrupt, as a young American. (He'd settle for sleeping with one, though.) But of course, it's also a song about his own damage. "Young Americans" is his testimony about the wages of being a poseur and the dangers of solipsism. Personality is a fun drug to fool around with, but too much of it can take a toll on your—well, let's call it your soul. "I'm a pretty cold person," Bowie told *Rolling Stone* in 1972. "A *very* cold person, I find." How can such a cold guy produce such emotional songs? "I'm not sure if that's really me coming through in the songs. They come out and I hear them afterward and I think, well, whoever wrote that really felt strongly about it. I *can't* feel strongly. I get so numb. I find that I'm walking around numb. I'm a bit of an iceman."

"Young Americans" is coming from the same place spiritually as Kanye West's "Bound 2," one of the great songs of this century and another lament from a coldhearted poseur mourning his failure to feel things authentically, obsessing over vintage soul music as a way he can share vicariously in actual laughter and tears. For Kanye it's the "uh-huh, honey" that loops through the song—the sampled voice of bona fide young American Brenda Lee, only fourteen when she uttered those words in her 1959 hit "Sweet Nothings." Kanye is haunted by that "uh-huh honey" because he can never live up to the openhearted sincerity of it, though her voice might be his shot at redemption.

For Bowie, looking out at the American kids in his audience, they're his shot at redemption, too. He craves an "uh-huh honey" to make him break down and cry. Like Kanye, he gets so tired of loving with nobody to love. He yearns to shake off his self-consciousness for a moment and lose himself to the song they're playing on the radio. You might suspect celebrity condescension here—superstars fetishizing how the common people live. Kanye thinks it's funny the girl in the club is wearing Forever 21 ("but just turned thir-*taaay*") like David digs the Afro-Sheen. Yet I don't hear a condescending moment in either song; there's a tremendous amount of respect in the way they refuse to bullshit about their distance from normal life. The girl paid to get in the club, Kanye didn't, he's not gonna pretend he doesn't like that. Bowie doesn't claim he took the bus to the studio. He isn't one of those English blues dudes getting back to roots that were never his. He's just passing through.

And he doesn't make any false claims about giving up being a poseur—are you kidding? That's a vice he likes way too much. All Bowie wants is to stay a phony forever, but also to have real feelings. Is that so much to ask?

BOWIE HAD A LOT TO SAY TO US YOUNG AMERICANS. He plucked us out from our daily milk-shake-drinking routine and put us in his musical fantasies. You might be stuck in the middle of nowhere, with no particular place to go, but you were *in this song*. Bowie looked at you and he didn't see a loser kid—he saw a passionate bright young thing. The "Rebel Rebel" girl isn't hot because of how she looks or what she owns but because of her desires—nothing exotic, just loud bands and dancing and terrifying her parents. But wanting it lights her up and makes her a transmission and a live wire.

Bowie's audience was his instrument. Ziggy really couldn't play guitar; what Ziggy played was the kids. Without us, he was nothing, and he knew it, and we, his believers, were the records the DJ played. "Lay the real thing on me," he pleaded, and we could because we *were* the real thing. (At least the girls were. It always seemed like the girls were realer than the boys, as far as Bowie was concerned. Part of being a boy in the Bowie universe is being cool with that.) He wanted some of what we had; we wanted loads of what he had.

Ever since he was a little kid, he fantasized about American realness. He panted over anything young and loud, and America was the place to find it—especially that city that so fascinates Europeans, Detroit, the realest of industrial hellholes. Iggy Pop was his personal ambassador to Detoilet, the city of noise, even if the Stooges were secretly from Ann Arbor. Detroit was also the home of Motown, which gave Bowie his title: label boss Berry Gordy decorated Motown singles with the slogan "The Sound of Young America." But most of all, it was the city of Aretha—it's odd how much the Queen of Soul haunts Bowie, especially in that *Cracked Actor* scene where he sings along with "(You Make Me Feel Like) A Natural Woman" with a sheepish grin, knowing he could never pass for either natural or a woman. He was visibly touched at the honor of handing her a Grammy—"La Supreme Femme Noir"—the night she said, "I could kiss David Bowie!" ("Which she didn't," he recalled in 1999, still disappointed decades later. "So I slunk off stage left.")

My favorite thing anybody ever said about Aretha Franklin comes from Luther Vandross, in 1982: "This woman ain't entertainment. She's done opened the books to my life and told everybody." No doubt that's how Bowie felt about Aretha, and he hoped we might feel that way about him, too. "Plastic soul" wasn't just a self-deprecating joke; he always liked hiding behind a plastic mask in order to express himself. (His first childhood instrument was a plastic sax.) His new phase was an attempt to salvage what was left of his own emotional realness, as in the ballad "Win," where he tells a special lady, "I've never touched you since I started to feel." For him, realness was whatever he wasn't enough of—that's why he kept trying on a variety of cultures, genders, ages, stepping into strangers' lives to ponder how music sounded to them. Not in an anthropological way, but in the spirit of Stevie Wonder pretending to be Jamaican or the Wu-Tang Clan pretending to be Sicilian or Stevie Nicks pretending to be a Welsh witch or Kurt Cobain pretending to be Stevie Nicks.

He wanted to reach out and touch the hearts of "Young Americans," and he did, though in ways he couldn't have dreamed possible. It makes a beautifully twisted kind of sense that "Young Americans" was the big break for Luther Vandross, the ultimate R&B love man, but at the time a complete unknown who dropped by the studio to visit his old school friend Carlos Alomar. "David overheard me singing a vocal idea of mine and immediately put me on the microphone," Luther recalled. "It was my first experience of recording and it cemented my desire to pursue a career in music." Bowie took him on tour as his opening act, but the first night, fans ignored him and shouted for the headliner. "Bowie said, 'Please. Later for these people. Later for them. You go out there and get your art together.'" Vandross hung in there—and Bowie introduced him to Bette Midler, who hired him next. A few years later, Luther was producing Aretha. Bowie's romance with R&B realness turned out to be a two-way street.

So "Young Americans" is a poseur's love song. Bowie is old enough to get the fear he'll never feel real himself. He's also old enough to fear he *will* get real, and then he'll get boring and miss out on all the pleasures of slinkily vagabonding. Church on time terrifies him. Bowie might not belong anywhere or to anyone. But he feels those flickers of desire, for a moment here and there, and that makes him feel as close to real as he'll get. Maybe it even makes him break down and cry.

THE PLASTIC
SOUL BROTHER

1975

Bowie finally topped the American charts with "Fame," his first Number 1 hit. He'd swanned through the Top 40 before— "Space Oddity" had made it to Number 15, while "Young Americans" stalled at Number 28. But the glam-disco strut of "Fame" whisked him to a whole new realm of mainstream celebrity. This song changed everything about the Bowie story: it turned a rocker into a pop darling and gave him a Middle American mass audience, and for an artist like Bowie, there was no chance he'd pass up the opportunity to play with this audience like a new toy. "It doesn't look good for America," he warned in 1975. "They let people like me trample all over their country." Before the year was out, he was lip-syncing "Fame" on *Soul Train*. Is it any wonder?

"Fame" was a quickie he slapped together with two new buddies. One knew a lot more about fame than he did: John

Lennon. As Bowie recalled, "Surrealistically enough, we were first introduced in about 1974 by Elizabeth Taylor." Lennon was in the midst of his drunken "lost weekend" phase, after Yoko had thrown him out. The not-so-famous collaborator was the young Harlem guitarist Carlos Alomar, who went on to become his longest-running musical wingman. Alomar was justifiably skeptical about the idea of Bowie faking the funk. As he says in the documentary *Five Years*, "This was the whitest man I've ever seen. I'm not talking about white like pink. I'm talking translucent white." Alomar took him to the Apollo Theater—and also took him home to fatten him up with soul food. "He was freaky. At one point I told him—and you'll have to excuse my language—'You look like shit, man. You need some food.'"

Bowie was none too subtle about his desire to hustle Lennon into the studio—teaming up with a Beatle would be the ultimate validation. After months of wooing, he got his chance. Alomar came up with the guitar riff, Lennon came up with the falsetto "*faaaame!*" squawk, somebody might have come up with a few drugs, and suddenly these gents found themselves ducking into a New York studio to bang out this disco track, along with a rough remake of the Beatles' "Across the Universe." "Fame" was plastic soul coated in *Rubber Soul*, a cheeky satire about a subject Bowie thought he already knew inside out, the mind-altering dangers of excess visibility. But he couldn't have been prepared for where this song would take him.

"Fame" would have been merely a worthy art project if it had sold modestly—as it did in his native land, where it barely dented the Top 20. Yet "Fame" became something different once the audience got hold of it—it turned out America loved hearing everybody's favorite pansexual extraterrestrial try to boogie down. Even Alomar's former boss James Brown thought this song was worth stealing. It just confirmed Bowie's longtime hunch that rock stars were lagging way behind the audience. "Trying to tart the rock business up a bit is getting nearer to what the kids themselves are like," he explained in his *Rolling Stone* sit-down with William S. Burroughs. "The kids are a lot more sensational than the stars themselves. The rock business is a pale shadow of what the kids' lives are usually like." The way he saw it, he was just trying to catch up with the fans. "Walk down Christopher Street and then you wonder exactly what went wrong. People are not like James Taylor; they may be molded on the outside, but inside their heads it is something completely different."

Then he set out to prove it, one flashbulb at a time. Now that he'd scored a Number 1 hit, he couldn't wait to turn into the kind of Hollywood star who cuddles with Liz Taylor for the paparazzi while assuring the Sunday papers they're just good friends, frolicking for the audience discovering him via *People* magazine, *American Top 40*, and daytime talk shows. This kind of fame was a whole new drug, and Bowie was not one to dabble discreetly. Hollywood's latest pet freak began boasting about his impending movie stardom, proclaiming, "I'm really just my own little corporation of characters."

Bowie was all over American TV in this period—since he was living in L.A., and since he was crazy high all the time, this was the year he chose to spend as much time as possible on camera. He went to *The Dick Cavett Show*, looking like a lacquered skeleton in suspenders and shoulder pads, stuffed into a brown tweed suit and trotted out for the camera as an impersonation of a live human—some kind of *Weekend at Bowie's* prank. He does "Fame" and the R&B oldie "Footstompin'" with a fierce dance break from his new twenty-two-year-old girlfriend Ava Cherry—though honestly, she seems like a bit of a workout for a man in Bowie's condition. His voice is shot to pieces, blowing note after note; Luther has a hard time keeping a straight face. The absurdly wasted Bowie also sits for a chat, sniffling, twiddling his cane and mumbling incoherent coke babble at his terrified host. As he admitted years later, "I didn't know where I was." But he flickers to life for a moment when discussing his fans, rejecting the suggestion that they're copying him. "I get influenced by people who come to see me," he insists. "It wasn't me, it was them."

This Bowie looks like a model of poise compared to the even

paler, twitchier, and clumsier model who sashayed immodestly onto the stage of *Soul Train*. It must have looked like a historic honor—the whitest human ever invited onto the show. (A title previously held by Elton John, who did a much kickier "Philadelphia Freedom" on *Soul Train* six months earlier.) Alas, Bowie wasn't feeling the funk that day. First there's an agonizing Q&A with the audience; Bowie mutters at the floor until a worried-looking Don Cornelius says, "Okay, David, I think we have to move on." Then he flinches his way through a valiant effort to lip-sync "Golden Years," even though he can't remember the words. "I hadn't bothered to learn it," Bowie confessed later. When he lurches into "Fame," he's expecting more applause from the audience than he gets, but fortunately, he's not awake enough to notice. Don Cornelius does *not* ask him to talk again.

He's a lot more together in his visits to Dinah Shore. Her format requires Bowie to sit quietly for minutes at a time and listen while her other guests do the talking, but he's startlingly good at it. His Royal Crackedness clearly woke up that morning and decided he wanted to try playing the role of a well-brought-up houseguest. He's deferential to Henry Winkler (later one of Morrissey's closest friends in L.A., so the Fonz has good taste in pasty Brits), and since Bowie was fond of describing himself as a sponge, he was probably also a fan of Nancy Walker's TV ads for Bounty paper towels; he, too, prided himself on being extra-absorbent. (Bowie: The Quicker Picker-Upper!) Later in the show he gets karate lessons—he handles it well until his instructor tries to teach him how to take a kick in the groin. Dinah held the record as Bowie's most old-school TV foil until a couple of years later, when he appeared on a sad little holiday special called *Bing Crosby's Merrie Olde Christmas*. He sang a fierce "'Heroes'" that day, but the program will always be remembered for the cross-generational money scene when Bowie knocks on Bing's door to sing a duet on "The Little Drummer Boy," even though neither man knew a thing about the other ("I just knew my mother liked him," Bowie said) or got the other's jokes. "Oh, I love modern music—I think some of it's *real* fine," Bing says, probably not thinking of "Diamond Dogs." It's a historic moment of cardigan-clad cheese. Bing dropped dead on the golf course a month later, before the special aired.

But the prize of all Bowie seventies TV moments is the *Cher* variety show, where two of the seventies' grooviest divas meet for a duet—possibly the most insane moment of either career. They start out with a hip-swinging rendition of "Young Americans" until they swerve into a chaotic oldies medley, doing nuggets by the Beatles, Buddy Holly, the Crystals, Neil Diamond, Three Dog Night, mostly just a line or two of the song before zooming on to the next one, to the point where Bowie's on his knees serenading Cher with the Chantels' doo-wop classic "Maybe." They're trying to sum up rock and roll history, tramping and thieving through the fifties and sixties, yet there's nothing not seventies about it, from the garish apricot-and-tinsel soundstage to the leading lady's fright wig. Bowie looks right at home in Cher World, rocking a leisure suit he boasted he'd found at Sears.

Give the man credit for not doing anything halfway. He jumped right into the deep end of the seventies celebrity grotto and made zero apologies. "I have no confidence in David Jones as a public figure," he told *People* readers. "Jones has become a real shell. He's given it all to Bowie." And who is Bowie? "He's like a Lego kit. I'm convinced I wouldn't like him, because he's too vacuous and undisciplined." A fitting seventies metaphor, though this Lego Soul Brother couldn't stay snapped together long. "Fame" proved to be even more toxic than he'd imagined, which might have been what John Lennon was trying to warn him about. "Fame puts you there where things are hollow"? He'd barely begun to see how hollow things could get.

THE MAN WHO
FELL TO EARTH

1976

Bowie's big shot at the movie career he craved was *The Man Who Fell to Earth* in 1976. It became his defining film role, inspired when director Nicolas Roeg saw the *Cracked Actor* documentary on television and realized he'd found the perfect creature to play an extraterrestrial stranded in the American desert. "My one snapshot memory of that film is not having to act," Bowie said in 1993. "I wasn't of this earth at that particular time."

Roeg set up a meeting at Bowie's apartment, but Bowie forgot all about it, so Roeg sat waiting patiently in Bowie's kitchen for eight hours until the Dame returned. Bowie was impressed by this show of determination. In truth, eight hours of sitting in Bowie's kitchen was undoubtably more thrilling than two hours of sitting through *The Man Who Fell to Earth*, but it's a film that provided visual elements of the Bowie mythology. He looks fantastic—the footage provided the photos for his next two album covers, *Station to Station* and *Low*. Roeg is a still photographer at heart, with a sense for how a movie can look but no interest in how a movie can move, so his films are basically slide shows that drag on forever. Mick Jagger and Anita Pallenberg in *Performance*, Jenny Agutter in *Walkabout*, Julie Christie in *Don't Look Now*—they all look exquisite, especially naked, yet even they look bored. The same goes for Bowie in this one.

The filming was in New Mexico, where Bowie took up with costume designer Ola Hudson, a black Angelena, and bonded with her eight-year-old son, Saul. The world would later know Saul under the name Slash, the guitarist in Guns N' Roses. But in 1975 he was just a kid meeting his mom's new boyfriend. "It was like watching an alien land in your backyard," Slash recalled years later. "My mother practiced the same form of transcendental meditation that David did. They chanted before the shrine she maintained in the bedroom." When David dropped by Ola's house, he used to bring Angie and Zowie, in true seventies let-it-all-hang-out style. "I sometimes used to put him to bed at nights, little Slash," Bowie said fondly in 2002. "Who'd have guessed?" Ola took Saul to see him at the L.A. Forum. "I saw the familiar elements of a man I'd gotten to know exaggerated to the extreme. He had reduced rock stardom to its roots: being a rock star is the intersection of who you are and who you want to be."

Bowie plays an ethereal creature who visits America so he can steal our water. ("We saw your planet on television. Our name for your planet means 'Planet of Water.'") However, he gets corrupted by his time in America, meets a dimwit woman, gets persecuted by the government, hides in a room full of TV screens, loses his ability to go back to his home planet and becomes an alcoholic. It's not one of those bad films that's fun to watch despite itself—it's quite unpleasant to spend time with. Candy Clark has "one of those voices that could peel paint off the wall," as Bowie said. The acting is so hammy, the plot twists so manipulative, the violence so sadistic, the special effects so chintzy. Then there's the Rip Torn full-frontal scene. (Rip ain't no Jenny Agutter, that's for sure.) Not even the music helps, beyond Ricky Nelson's "Hello Mary Lou." Bowie wanted to do the soundtrack himself, but when he couldn't get it together in time, they called in the Mamas and the Papas' John Phillips, the famous Wolf King of L.A., not to mention one of rock's most notorious opiate hounds. How is it possible to get so flaked out that John Phillips looks like the reliable pro? Funniest moment: someone takes a look at Bowie and says, "You know, mister, I don't think you get enough to eat."

But Bowie looks magnificent through it all, a flash of orange hair against the washed-out desert landscape. He's the only sign of life, not that he retained many memories of the film shoot. Asked about it in 2002, he said, "Did the film work come next? Ah, you tell me! Possibly! I know I had a lovely hat. It was *that* period. A fedora: the Borsalino." It's a Bowie-as-Messiah movie, an allegory about a dreamboat too pure and noble for a planet that didn't deserve him. "There's true insolence in Bowie's lesbian-Christ leering," Pauline Kael said in her review. "Lighted like the woman of mystery in thirties movies, he's the most romantic figure in recent pictures—the modern version of the James Dean lost-boy myth."

The final scene is our defeated Bowie in despair in his Borsalino, mourning that he'll never see his wife again. He can only communicate with her via his music—so he makes an album for her, *The Visitor*. This is the first time in the movie we find out this alien is a musician. How did he learn how to make an album? What does it sound like? What instruments does he play? Or does he sing? Why hasn't his music been integrated into any other part of the story? We never find out. But what a final image: Bowie reduced to hoping this album gets played on the radio, so the waves will travel through space, and on some nearby planet, his wife's radio will pick up a bit of noise and she'll recognize it as him.

Despite some warm reviews, this was the project where Bowie seemed to figure out the movies were too tiny for him. He'd already proved rock and roll was the place for an imagination as unruly as his. After this star turn, he mostly aimed for smaller roles on the art fringes, doing well-regarded bits as Andy Warhol in *Basquiat* and Pontius Pilate in Martin Scorsese's *The Last Temptation of Christ*. He'd hoped to be a matinee idol, but he couldn't, because rock stars are just cooler than actors, and it's not the kind of cool Bowie could tone down or turn off at will. That's where rock movies always fail—no actor is cool enough to play the part. And that's why nobody could make a movie about Bowie, because no actor could contain him—not even Bowie the Actor. Nick Cave, who knows his way around films, books, and other media, once explained to me how it works. "The more attention you absorb, the more monstrous you become," he said. "It's almost exclusively a rock-star thing. Actors can duck and dive a bit—they constantly re-create themselves. All they can do is *play* the role of a monster. But nobody does monster like a rock star."

And no rock star does monster like Bowie. The real high point of his film career is *The Hunger*, his shamefully underrated 1983 vampire flick with Catherine Deneuve and Susan Sarandon. (Why, yes—the ladies *do* make out. How did you guess?) Stevie Nicks told me in 2014 that *The Hunger* was her favorite moment of his career. "I'm a big fan of David Bowie—especially his movie *The Hunger*. Just creepy and strange and amazingly beautiful. I'm always surprised Bowie didn't make more vampire movies." The film is a sacred text of goth culture, especially the opening ten minutes: Bowie and Deneuve cruise a New York goth club, where the children of the night groove to Bauhaus playing "Bela Lugosi's Dead." They move through the dance floor, prowling for some nubile human flesh to suck dry. They lure a foxy black-leather couple back to their alcove for a night of sin. The Bauhaus song builds as the vampires pair off with their delectable human guests. Bowie undresses the girl (the not-yet-famous Ann Magnuson) in the kitchen. Deneuve towers over the boy by the fireplace, her ice-queen black shades still on. That's when the fangs come out. Undead, undead, undead.

THE THIN WHITE DUKE

1976

On the cover of the *Rolling Stone*, February 1976: Bowie stares into the distance under an orange pompadour that probably weighs more than the rest of him does. He later revealed the photo was snapped while he was holding a handgun, doing some target practice in L.A. "The gun was a present from one of my mid-seventies 'friends.' I was definitely under the impression that I was merely 'passing through this world.' I didn't care where I came from and cared less where I was going. The present was futile and surreal. I ate little, but ingested a critically unfair amount of chemicals."

It was obviously time for this Visitor to get out of town. In the immortal words of Gladys Knight and the Pips, L.A. proved too much for the man. Bowie had become such a Hollywood fixture, Joni Mitchell could mock him for hanging around too much in "The Hissing of Summer Lawns." ("A diamond dog carrying a cup and a cane," that's harsh. But fair.)

Yet before Bowie pulled himself out of the oxygen tent called America, he had one last statement to make. The whole sordid story of 1970s rock can be heard in the grooves of *Station to Station*: Europe's glam starlet lost out west, sampling the local pharmaceuticals, stir-frying what's left of his mind, dubbing himself the Thin White Duke. This robot-funk space-rock epic holds up as his greatest album, even if he couldn't remember making it. "I remember working with Earl [Slick] on the guitar sounds," he said in 1997. "And that's about all I remember of it. I can't even remember the studio. I know it was in L.A. because I've read it was in L.A."

The Thin White Duke is the villain Bowie plays in these songs: a European aristocrat cad with slicked-down blond hair, a black waistcoat, and a sepulchral bel canto voice. Bowie called him "a would-be romantic with absolutely no emotion." The Duke was a character Bowie used to explore his mystical obsessions, especially the kabbalah—on the back cover of later reissues, he sits on the floor drawing a diagram of the Sefirot, while he sings about the emanations of divine energy: "Here we are, one magical movement from Kether to Malkuth," the opposite ends of the kabbalistic Tree of Life. He ponders the Stations of the Cross, a Catholic devotion I know well, and spinning the radio dial, a mystic ritual I know even better. He speeds through railway and radio stations, losing himself in the tunnels of his overheated brain. He reads a lot of paper-

1970. *Photo by Hulton Archive/Getty Images*

1972. *Photo by Michael Ochs Archives/Getty Images*

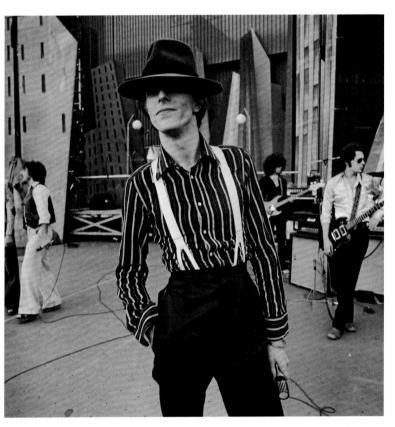

1974. *Photo by Terry O'Neill/Getty Images*

1975. *Photo by Ron Galella/WireImage*

1976. *Photo by Michael Ochs Archives/Getty Images*

1978. *Photo by Bob Riha, Jr./Getty Images*

1983. *Photo by Greg Gorman/Contour by Getty Images*

1995. *Photo by Kevin Cummins/Getty Images*

backs about the occult and black magic. And most important, he stumbles into a rock and roll band, the best one he ever assembled, which is the reason all the psychodramas of this album come across loud and clear.

Bowie's breakdowns in this period have long been the stuff of legend: a paranoid recluse hiding in his mansion, staying up for days at a time on Peruvian flake, fretting about witches stealing his bodily fluids, burning black candles, keeping his urine bottled in the fridge to ward off evil spells, living on raw peppers and milk. But the real document we have of this period— the evidence we have to go on—is the music, which is full of vitality and humor, even at its most deranged. It's possible the witches and peppers have been overpublicized; it's undeniable his rhythm section has been underpublicized. And they're the heroes of this album, not to mention the heroes of *"Heroes."* Bowie's five best albums came all in a five-year rush: *Station to Station* (1976), *Low* (1977), *"Heroes"* (1977), *Lodger* (1979), *Scary Monsters* (1980). What do these albums have in common? The rhythm section: Dennis Davis on drums, George Murray on bass, and Carlos Alomar on guitar. They're the guys who worked on all five. And they're why these records don't sound like other music by Bowie or anyone else—listen to what Davis, Alomar, and Murray are doing in "Stay" or "Blackout" or "Golden Years" or "Sound and Vision." The heart of the pentalogy is this trio, who were maybe not the most publicity-hungry musicians he ever worked with, and so haven't gotten their share of the glimmer.

There were other crucial collaborators in this period. Tony Visconti produced four of these albums; Brian Eno played on three of them. Robert Fripp played on a couple. You can't imagine *Low* without Ricky Gardiner's guitar or *Lodger* without Adrian Belew's. But the Davis/Murray/Alomar axis was one of the toughest rock and roll bands that ever existed. Davis and Murray were jazz guys who'd played with the likes of Roy Ayers and Weldon Irvine; Davis drummed on the soundtrack of the Pam Grier blaxploitation classic *Coffy*. "Dennis was so open," Bowie recalled in 1997. "He was almost orgiastic in his approach to trying out new stuff. He'd say, 'Yeah, let's do that new shit, man.' I told him about a Charlie Mingus gig that I saw where the drummer had polythene tubes that would go into the drums, and he would suck and blow to change the pressure as he played. Dennis was out the next day buying that stuff. Dennis is crazy, an absolute loony man, but he had a lot of his own thoughts on things, and he would throw us all kinds of curveballs." In a way, the Davis/Murray/Alomar trio are like the quartet who backed Rod Stewart on his early solo records—they never had a name, they were never officially a band, but they're why you can still hear "Maggie May" on the radio every day.

The Thin White Duke's new songs were ominous, yet also

the funniest he'd ever done, especially when he yelps, "It's not the side effects of the cocaine—I'm thinking that it must be *loooove!*" Producer Harry Maslin, who'd just engineered a Number 1 pop hit with Barry Manilow's "Mandy," gives the whole album a massive sound, with piano propulsion from Roy Bittan of Bruce Springsteen's E Street Band. (Which is why Bruce's "Candy's Room" weirdly sounds like it belongs on this album.) The Duke spends most of *Station to Station* brooding over rueful romance, from the first-kiss jitters of "Stay" to the promise of "Golden Years." And then there's "TVC15." As Bowie told the Long Island crowd that March, "This is a love story between a girl and her television set." Frank Sinatra visited the studio and gave his blessing to Bowie's version of the Hollywood torch song "Wild Is the Wind." The sessions would start around midnight, then keep going—three days? Four days? Who could tell? "I'd stay up for weeks," he said later. "Even people like Keith Richards were floored by it. And there were pieces of me all over the floor." When he wasn't ranting to his dealers and groupies about the Golden Dawn or the Holy Grail, he hired a white witch to fly in from New York and perform an exorcism on his swimming pool. He was truly a walking study in demonology.

But all his cosmic dabblings come together in the ten-minute title epic. As he told *Q* in February 1997, "The 'Station to Station' track itself is very much concerned with the Stations of the Cross. All the references within the piece are to do with the Kabbalah. It was the nearest album to a magick treatise that I've ever written. I've never read a review that sussed it. It's an extremely dark album. Miserable time to live through, I must say."

"STATION TO STATION" IS A GARGANTUAN VERSION of that R&B standby, the train song. All aboard: it begins with locomotive sound effects, then Earl Slick's guitar feedback, and we're back on James Brown's night train, except instead of Baltimore, Richmond, Atlanta, Miami, this train is rolling from Kether to Malkuth to the outlands of Judaic/Christian/gnostic mysticism. Yet the longer it builds, and the heavier the guitar gets, James Brown is always on board this train, along with all the other theosophical baggage Bowie has brought along, and as the wheels pick up speed, so does Bowie—in the final minutes, he's walking on air while the band walks it home. With all due respect to his occult Arthurian totalitarian numerology, it's a mystic realm he couldn't get near without his drummer.

After three minutes of his "Night Train," James Brown calls "Carry me home," but Bowie's got a longer ride ahead of him. The train keeps rolling all night long, trouble ahead, trouble behind, as the whole band drives like a demon, hitting the cities JB shouts out in "Night Train"—the piano so New Orleans, the guitar so New York. There's an ominous sense of homecoming, as he announces, "The European canon is here," but his all-American musicians keep escalating the groove, making it all bigger and louder as if they're trying to rush through all the Kabbalistic spheres. (There are ten of those; the song runs ten minutes.) The vehicle blasts through the stations without slowing down, the scenery a blur. You realize you're trapped on a crazy train with a phantom engineer—Davy Jones as Casey Jones—who has no idea you can't drive from L.A. to Europe. Yet the pleasure of the groove is so intense, you're glad to ride it out to the end. I never play this song without wanting to hear the whole thing again.

The Stations of the Cross are a devotional meditation on fourteen steps along Jesus's march to death, a death he freely accepted, some based on incidents in the canonical Bible (Jesus is condemned to crucifixion by Pilate, who Bowie would later play in a movie), others from Catholic tradition (a woman named Veronica steps forward to wipe his face as he carries his cross). Nothing arcane about the Stations—they're displayed prominently along the walls of virtually all Catholic churches. Veronica's napkin was fabled to bear the image of Jesus's face. It makes sense this image of groupie-saint hagiography would prove attractive to a rock star like Bowie; he'd already written a great song about being redeemed by the adoration of a Veronica in "Growing Up and I'm Fine," a gem he donated to Mick Ronson's solo LP. To participate in the Stations is to leave the written scriptures behind and enter the Christ story yourself, which is why it can be a frightening devotion to practice (or to some non-Catholic Christians, a blasphemously pagan one). So it's easy to see why it appealed to Bowie, at a time when he was burning black candles and drawing pentagrams all over his walls. He was walking his own personal Via Dolorosa, and in his peppers-and-milk paranoia, he was devouring every scrap of spiritual scripture he could get his hands on. At one point he chants "It's too late to be hateful"—which sounds like a bit of wisdom he might have picked up from that ancient esoteric text "Uncle John's Band," by the Grateful Dead.

Kabbalah was enjoying a trendy cachet in those post-hippie days. Harold Bloom usefully explained Western culture's infatuation in the mid-1970s, around the time Bowie was making this record: "Popular Kabbalism has understood, somehow, that the Sefirot are neither *things* nor *acts*, but rather are *relational events*, and so are persuasive representations of what ordinary people encounter as the inner reality of their lives." That's definitely true of Bowie. Moving from Kether to Malkuth means descending from the crown of creation (the divine source beyond human comprehension) to the earthly kingdom (the material world that reflects God's glory). In other words, falling to earth.

"Station to Station" steals another classic James Brown trick—the stage routine where his handlers come out to wrap a robe around the man's shoulders and lead him offstage, but he fights his way back to the microphone for just one more chorus, until his handlers try to drag him away again. "Station to Station" keeps thundering on for one more chorus, long past the point where you think it's going to fade out. But the train never gets home. It's too late.

AS FAR AS HIS NEW POP AUDIENCE WAS CONCERNED, *Station to Station* was a de facto second album from the star who'd captured a new audience with "Fame" the previous year. It was a commercial smash, reaching Number 3 on the charts while "Golden Years" became a Top 10 single. The 1976 Isolar tour was one of his most acclaimed—Bowie in stark white light, dandied up as the Duke in white shirt and black waistcoat (an outfit designed by Ola Hudson), only five musicians behind him, the only stage prop the blue Gitanes pack tucked into his pocket. He began the show with the infamous 1929 surrealist silent film *Un Chien Andalou*, which simulates an act of gory violence (slicing an eyeball); he knew it was time to walk to the stage when he heard the audience gasp. When Bowie covers Lou Reed's "I'm Waiting for the Man," yelping "twenty-six dollars in my hand," that sounds like it wouldn't even cover his drug budget for the next five minutes. In bootleg videos of the tour, he's every inch the Duke, living out Oscar Wilde's words in "The Philosophy of Dress": "The imagination will concentrate itself upon the waistcoat. Waistcoats will show whether a man can admire poetry or not. That will be very valuable. By a single glance one can detect the presence of the tedious."

On this tour, Bowie got busted for the first time, in the upstate New York city of Rochester (of all places), for marijuana (of all drugs), with Iggy and a couple of hangers-on. It wasn't his weed. "Bloody potheads," he groused. Given Bowie's taste in substances at the time (he liked to boast he wasn't into "slow drugs"), this was a lucky break; charges were dismissed. The bust was notable mostly for the glam mug shot, which surfaced three decades later in a retired cop's estate sale: Bowie looks sexier in his Rochester police-station snap than any other rock star looks at a big-money photo session.

Bowie's late-seventies journey has deep parallels with Marvin Gaye's—a couple of veteran stars adrift in the decade, bored with the way their peers are going through the motions, going off the deep end in L.A. mansions, living lavish lifestyles despite ruinous financial problems and marital breakdown and endless meetings with lawyers and the side effects of the cocaine. Gaye released "Got to Give It Up" a year after Bowie released "Station to Station"—two long grooves stretching into double-digit minutes, blatantly unconventional, with quizzical vocals and rubberband-man bass and hypnotically repetitive rhythm, going for synthetic effects while rejecting any kind of laid-back comforts. These records were a fuck-you to all the musicians their age who were content to play it safe and pander to the audience. But they were also a challenge to young listeners to catch up with the sound of the future, contemplating personal disasters with a hilariously spaced just-visiting-this-planet vibe.

When Gaye got handed a whopping alimony bill from the judge, he made a concept album about his divorce designed specifically to pay off his wife, calling it *Here, My Dear*. It's his Berlin trilogy in one double-vinyl album. They both complain about their superstar hassles, whether it's Bowie's "You're such a wonderful person but you've got problems" or Gaye's "Somebody tell me please why I have to pay attorney fees." Gaye complains about "blowin' coke all up my nose" and "foolin' round with midnight hoes." But they're testifying about the same midlife malaise. (And probably a few of the same midnight hoes.)

The Thin White Duke remains an icon of L.A. alienation—memorably evoked by the Red Hot Chili Peppers in their best song, "Californication," when they ask the ghost of Kurt Cobain if he can hear the spheres playing songs off *Station to Station*. But Bowie's farewell to L.A. was an appropriately melodramatic mess. "My least favorite city, I'm afraid," he said at the end of the seventies. "I really loathe it with a vengeance." He returned to play L.A. seven years later, on the 1983 Serious Moonlight tour. He pointedly began the show with "Look Back in Anger."

THE DICTATOR

1976

Bowie arrived at London's Victoria Station on May 2, 1976, a publicity event packed with journalists, photographers, and fans. He waved to the crowd for less than a minute, then disappeared. This was the day he gave the famous nonexistent Nazi salute, a hoax that dogged him for the rest of his life. You still see it mentioned often now, after his death. Just to be clear: nobody there saw Bowie make a Nazi salute. None of the newspaper reports of this event mentioned any Nazi salutes. Although the event was heavily photographed (that was the point), none of the photographers got any pictures of a Nazi salute.

Six days later, on May 8, the *NME* ran a photo that caught Bowie's arm in midwave at a funny angle, so they gave it the comedy caption "Heil and Farewell." Obviously, they weren't trying to accuse Bowie of really giving a Nazi salute. The accompanying article, by *NME* reporter Tony Stewart, made no mention of any Nazi salute—he mostly just complained that

Bowie didn't sing. But that's when this myth started. If Bowie had made a Nazi salute that day, he would have raised his right arm, which is how Nazi salutes are done. (He was waving with his left—customary for him, since he was left-handed.) But more important, if Bowie had saluted, somebody would have noticed at the time, or gotten it on film. This didn't happen. In the intervening six days, Bowie wasn't exactly low profile—in fact, he did a number of sold-out shows at Wembley Arena. If he wanted to give any kind of salute at all, he had plenty of opportunities. While he was in London that week, he might even have visited his mother. (Although he probably didn't. He was kind of a dick back then.)

But of course, the nonexistent salute just symbolized a deeper sickness in the Bowie psyche. People believed the Nazi hoax because he was saying all sorts of stupid shit in the press for attention, and it jolted him into realizing (finally) he had a deadly addiction to attention, not to mention a possibly as-deadly addiction to the same drug that made the Nazis think it was a clever idea to invade Russia. Earlier in 1976, he made comments that sounded fascistic in separate interviews, to Cameron Crowe (in *Rolling Stone* and *Playboy*) and to a Swedish reporter in Stockholm. In the Crowe interviews, he's obviously saying it for pure comic effect ("I'd be an excellent dictator"), prefacing them by fretting he hasn't said anything outrageous enough for Crowe to use. At the end of the *Playboy* interview,

Crowe asks if Bowie stands by what he's said. "Everything but the inflammatory remarks."

The Stockholm comment from April 26 sounds more earnest, therefore uglier. "As I see it, I am the only alternative for the premier in England. I believe Britain could benefit from a fascist leader. I mean fascist in its true sense, not Nazi. After all, fascism is really nationalism." The first sentence makes it clear this is an attempt at a joke, unless you seriously believe Bowie was planning to run for prime minister of a country he hadn't visited in two years. But if you drop the first sentence from that quote, it looks truly vile, so naturally that's what much of the press did (and still does). It seems like a case of Bowie's camp wit, a touch drier than usual, evading the Swedish sense of humor. But still, it's hard to have much sympathy for his plight. You hop around saying things like this, you can't whimper about bad publicity when people quote your words out of context. Live by the Nazi joke, die by the Nazi joke.

Bowie was shocked at how evil those words looked in print, and immediately began denouncing them. By May 2, when he made the salute that never really happened but was heard round the world anyway, he was already distancing himself from his fascistic comments of a few days earlier. And for the first time in his career, he wanted to explain himself. He told the *Daily Express*, "If I said it—and I've a terrible feeling I did say something like it to a Stockholm journalist who kept asking me political questions—I'm astounded anyone could believe it. I have to keep reading it to believe it myself. I'm not sinister." The reporter makes an urbane quip: "So long as it's publicity, does it matter?" Bowie isn't amused. "Yes, it does. It upsets me. Strong I may be. Arrogant I may be. Sinister I'm not." He repudiated his remarks clearly and forcefully, and kept doing so for decades afterward, though it's noteworthy (and admirable, in my opinion) that he never tried to claim he was misquoted. He did, however, deny making the Nazi salute—he denied it at the time and denied it for the rest of his life. As far as I can tell, it's the *only* stupid thing Bowie ever denied doing. So that carries some weight. What carries more weight is that the evidence backs him up.

But he was horrified at how eagerly people wanted to believe it was true, and that made him wonder what he was turning into. It wasn't unusual for Brits of his generation to have a queasy sense of humor about Nazi Germany, whether that's Keith Moon wearing an SS uniform or Peter Cook making Nazi salutes during his good-night waves on *SNL* or John Lennon lobbying to put Hitler on the cover of *Sgt. Pepper*. But it *was* unusual for people to take it as evidence of actual Nazi sympathies, especially after Bowie had made his share of anti-Nazi comments in the past. (Just a year earlier, he'd called one of his *Young Americans* songs a warning against impending fascist tyranny: "Watch out mate, Hitler's on his way back.")

As far as Britain's real-life fascists in the National Front party were concerned, Bowie's comments were neither evil nor a joke, and they embraced him, which horrified him as well. As he sang in "It's No Game," "To be insulted by these fascists is so degrading." He could no longer ignore that something was very wrong.

The *Daily Express* reporter asks what he thinks of the "quiet, shy" David Jones he used to be. "I liked him," Bowie says. "I still like him if I could only get in touch with him. We've been apart for a long time."

THE LOW PROFILE

1977

"I blew my nose one day and half my brains came out." With these gentle words, David Bowie said farewell to L.A., where he'd spent the mid-seventies buried up to his clavicle in white powder, and fled back to Europe for some personal detox. He moved to Berlin and rented himself a cold-water flat on the second floor above an auto-parts store. He cut his hair, gave away his fancy clothes, and walked around his Turkish neighborhood unrecognized. By day he went to the library or to coffee bars. By night he watched *Starsky and Hutch* with his sidekick of choice, Iggy Pop. That might sound like a strange companion for a journey that involves trying to upgrade your sobriety level. But in L.A., Iggy had been locked in a UCLA mental ward. Bowie was the only friend who came to visit him. (Of course, the first thing Bowie said to Iggy in the hospital was, "Want some blow?")

Berlin was a place for them both to hide away. "Artists need a place like that, because we're dangerous people," Iggy told me in 2009. "In my case, that's a great excuse for my twisted personality—hey, I'm artistic, that's why I'm such an asshole!" While Bowie was hitting bottom in L.A., Iggy had turned into a pariah, earning a rep as one of the music world's most pitiful dope casualties. "Lonesome days," he calls them. "When I was living this meandering, itinerant, peripatetic, Daniel Boone/Lewis and Clark kind of life, wandering from town to town. Although in my case it was lonesome because for years the rap on me was 'Don't let him in your house! He's a junkie! He's *insaaaane!*'"

Iggy had always been a dangerous guy to keep around. "It was always that way, from the very early days of the Stooges. Man, did we upset the whole neo-buckskin establishment. Every time we played, they'd look really worried, like, 'These guys are gonna fuck up our pot business. Get them out of here!' I always knew, unquestioningly, we were fucking great, and I knew the world would recognize. I just didn't know it would take thirty-five years. I guess me and society kind of met halfway—I got closer to normal, and the world got Iggier."

The world was no Iggier in 1977, and he and Bowie made an appropriately odd pair in Berlin—in a way, Iggy was an amulet Bowie could keep around to make sure normal people didn't get too close. He needed a little distance to do the musical woodshedding he wanted to try. They made *The Idiot* together at warp speed, as a dry run for the ideas Bowie would try out on *Low*. Bowie played most of the instruments, while Iggy improvised the lyrics on the mike. Bowie also went on Iggy's tour, strictly as a sideman, playing keyboards; he sat head down at the side of the stage, his cloth cap on, lurking behind his piano and a glass of beer. He revisited Dinah Shore and this time brought Iggy with him; like Bowie, Iggy showed remarkable manners and respect for Dinah, treating her to a Mae West–like vamp through "Sister Midnight" and "Funtime." Then they dashed off another Ig record, *Lust for Life*. Iggy played the role of Bowie's punk conscience, Hutch to his Starsky, as well as the wild American side of his still-raging ego. Iggy in a typical 1979 coke rant: "I've met all the women, and I'll tell you one thing, I'm more woman than any of 'em. I'm a real woman, because I have love, dependability, I'm good, kind, gentle, and I've the power to give real love. Why else would you think that such a strong man as David Bowie would be close to me? He's a real man, and I'm a real woman. Just like Catherine Deneuve."

Berlin wasn't quite a drug-detox retreat—although Bowie left the worst excesses behind in L.A., he was boozing heavily. But it was liberating in terms of his daily routine. "I've grown my hair back to mouse," he announced. "I'm even practicing walking down the street. Every day, I get up more nerve and try to be more normal and be less insulated against real people." The new David Bowie: the girl with the mousy hair. But he needed a relatively uncluttered life where people weren't paying so much attention to him, because he needed to start attending to some of the damage cocaine and celebrity had wreaked inside his head. As he recalled later, "For the first two or three years afterward, while I was living in Berlin, I would have days when things were moving in the room, and this was when I was totally straight."

LOW PRESENTS BOWIE AT THIRTY, IN ALL HIS CONTRA-dictions: artist, hedonist, introvert, astral traveler, sexual tourist, depressive, con man, charmer, liar. *Low*, released in January 1977, was a new beginning for Bowie, kicking off what is forever revered as his "Berlin trilogy," despite the fact that *Low* was mostly recorded in France. Side 1 consists of seven fragments, some manic synth pop songs, some just chilly atmospherics. Side 2 has four brooding electronic instrumentals. Both sides glisten with ideas: listening to *Low*, you hear Kraftwerk and Neu, maybe some Ramones, loads of Abba and disco. But *Low* flows together as an intensely emotional whole, as he moves through some serious psychic wreckage.

For the first time since he became a star, Bowie made an album with no title track, which means no title character to hide behind, and like *Hunky Dory*, his last LP without a leading man, *Low* marks a turning point in his life. The cover has his profile under the word *Low*, as in Low Profile, showing the world his right eye while keeping his other one (the permanently dilated one) unseen on the other side of his face, the dark side of the moon, taking in the surreal orange sky behind him. His collar is turned up against the wind. I used to wear a pin on my sweater with that Bowie head shot on it; what continually impressed me is how people could recognize that shade of orange from across a room. Low Orange is a color that doesn't exist elsewhere in nature. If you notice it when you see it, you're probably a Bowie freak.

Bowie had never made noises that sounded like this, and neither had anyone else. Brian Eno told me in 2014, at his London studio, about a friend from art school who said, "'If you want to do something original, do something difficult.' He covered an entire house in ball-point pen marks. That was original. And it was difficult." That's what happened on *Low*.

Eno looms large on *Low*—not only did he play keyboards on six of the eleven tracks and cowrite "Warszawa," but you can hear the influence of his own records, especially *Another Green World*. He and Bowie had become thick as thieves, bonding over a mutual love of electronic artists like Kraftwerk and composers like Steve Reich. Eno had a similarly restless attention span. "The time to make something is when the energy's up. I bore very quickly. I can't be bothered to do things over. It's not out of some sense of nobility and commitment and progress—it's just that I want to keep myself interested. I tire quickly of things that are too coherent." He encouraged Bowie's experimental new direction. "It's easy for people to become slaves of their success—essentially, people trust in more of the same. They don't trust the idea that going somewhere completely different can be just as good. So it can be refreshing when they meet someone who says, 'That one is weird—I like *that* one.' When an idea is new it's vulnerable, it's quite clumsy."

Bowie assembled a cast of characters who could bring these clumsy new ideas to life—especially producer Tony Visconti, who warped the guitars of Ricky Gardiner and Carlos Alomar, and distorted Dennis Davis's snare to create one of rock's all-time most-imitated drum sounds. (As Joy Division's Stephen Morris said a few years later, "We kept asking the engineer to make the drums sound like 'Speed of Life.' Strangely enough he couldn't.") Bowie and Eno called Visconti in New York to ask him to come produce this nutty record they wanted to make. "They asked me what sonically I could bring to the table, and I told them about this new gadget I had just bought, the Eventide Harmonizer. They asked what it did, and I said, it fucks with the fabric of time." It was the perfect band for fucking with space as well as time—as Visconti pointed out, the musicians came from around the world. "The rhythm section was from New York and L.A. Roy Young on piano was from England via Hamburg, and Brian Eno was from some strange galaxy.

I come from Brooklyn and David from Brixton. This wasn't your average garage band of neighborhood kids." In the music, every place gets visited and every place gets left.

The album was banged out in three weeks—the band dashed off the rhythm tracks in five days, mostly first takes that were intended as demos until Bowie and Visconti realized this was turning into the actual album. The record company begged Bowie not to release *Low*, but it became a surprise hit, reaching Number 2 on the UK charts and Number 11 in the States. "Sound and Vision" even made the British Top 10. "An ultimate retreat song," Bowie called it. "I was going through dreadful times. It was wanting to be put in a little cold room with omnipotent blue on the walls and blinds on the windows."

It was the Berlin Bowie, rather than the Ziggy Bowie, who became the man's most influential incarnation. Not just the way he used electronics, or how he mixed the drums, but the way he lived out every musician's fantasy—blowing up your career, stepping away from your image, going strictly on your nerve, starting over and emerging stronger than ever. And in an accidental case of canny timing, he did it in the year of punk, while bands like the Clash and the Pistols were slaying their elders. Bowie was now the last of the seventies rock stars who didn't look like a dinosaur, challenging himself and his audience with music that pushed as hard as the garageland bands did. The fact that people actually bought it was an unexpected bonus. Naturally, he celebrated by rushing right back into the studio. Bowie was getting cocky in Berlin—he knew he was making the music of his life, and he knew he'd caught a lucky break escaping the celebrity blackout. He grew a mustache to pass incognito through the streets by day; after hours he'd join Iggy to soak in pilsner at the local taverns. As Iggy later recalled, in a typical week they'd spend two days drunk, two days nursing their hangovers, and three days straight—"which is a pretty good balance for musicians."

He dropped *"Heroes"* in October, capping his 1977 as one of the most fruitful years any rock star ever had. Cerebral guitar god Robert Fripp flew in for the sessions and went straight from the airport to the studio that night with guitar in hand. Bowie, Eno, and Visconti figured he might as well plug in. A few hours later, he'd completed all his solos for the album, improvising along with each song the first time he heard it. For the title track, Fripp played a few different takes that Visconti layered together, while Eno filtered the guitar through his synthesizer. Then Fripp packed up his ax and went home. (He also posed for photos that night with Eno and Bowie—the comical arrogance of Bowie's face, head held so high his chin is pointing at the camera, says a lot about why this whole album worked out so well.)

"'Heroes'" is the most beloved song from his Berlin years, as it deserves to be—along with "Space Oddity," it's the one everybody knows, even if they barely recognize Bowie's name. He sets the scene over a majestic Velvet Underground guitar-and-piano clang: Two lovers share a fleeting moment together, a kiss under the shadow of the Berlin Wall. The guards shoot over their heads to scare them off. The lovers wish they could meet in a place where they both belong. They wish they had a better world to share. But they're not retreating from this one. They trudge though a dirty and divided city to the place where they meet. They'll always have this kiss. They can be heroes, just for one day.

"'Heroes'" came from a break in the sessions at Hansa Studios, when Bowie took a stroll and spotted a couple by the Wall. It was only years later, after "'Heroes'" became a standard, that he confessed he knew who these lovers were: he'd accidentally busted his producer Tony Visconti sneaking off for a snog with one of the backup singers. But to him, the people sharing this kiss really are heroes, despite the ironic quotation marks he puts around the title. As he put it at the time, "The only heroic act one can fucking well pull out of the bag in a situation like that is to get on with life and derive some joy from the very simple pleasure of remaining alive, despite every attempt being made to kill you." And he tells their story with a romantic fire in his throat, living up to every Sinatra aspiration he ever had. It's the opposite of the Major Tom fantasy—instead of escaping to a bluer sky, it's about two people toughing it out down here, in a world ruled by bad men whom nothing will drive away. They might be a couple traveling through the years together; they might be strangers. This kiss will end, and the Wall will still be there, so will the guards and guns, so will the bills to be paid and the kids to be fed. But right now, they're lovers and that is that.

THE DJ

1979

The radio DJ sits at his console, behind glass. Stacks of records. Two turntables and a microphone. An antenna somewhere far away. He sits in his solitary late-night studio and plays the records, like the alien at the end of *The Man Who Fell to Earth*, hoping there's a girl somewhere listening. The music churns and swirls, a violin solo that doesn't sound like a violin surging while Bowie trills at the top of his register. The chorus: "I am a DJ. I am what I play." I was in eighth grade when this song came out, and it became a lifelong favorite. I could tell Bowie was satirizing the DJ's megalomania, as he shrieks, "I've got believers!" (The concept of satirizing things is so key when you're thirteen.) But it wasn't really an exaggeration. I was thirteen and discovering Bowie on the radio. I really did love the DJs. I was proud to be part of that invisible audience. I believed in them like I believed in Bowie. He is the DJ, we are what he plays.

The DJ in this song gets off on having believers, but to my teen self, that never seemed like an extravagant claim for a DJ to make. My mentors in Bowieism were the DJs on Boston rock radio, first WCOZ and then WBCN. I can't remember my current Netflix password, but I can tell you the number of the 'BCN listener line, 536-8000. I used to call to make requests, but more important, when I desperately wanted to know the name of the song the DJ was playing, before it slipped away. What if I never hear it again? Who's singing? What's it called?

"This song?" the kid on the other end of the line would say. (Never the DJ, alas.) "It's called 'Changes.' You know, that's why it goes 'ch-ch-ch-ch-changes' through the whole song?" Hey, sorry, guy—just making sure. The record stores are full of kids searching in vain for a Zeppelin song called "You Don't Have to Go." The DJ is the guy who has to tell you the joke about Jamaica.

A radio station—that's where the music was back then. The DJs got to sit in the sacred room full of vinyl, keepers of the keys of rock and roll wisdom. All these years later, I remember their names and their voices and their time slots and their tastes. Lisa Karlin's favorite song was the Motels' "Total Control." Carmelita's favorite song was "More Than This." Charles Laquidara, every morning. Carter Alan, every night. Ken Shelton, Steven Clean, Razz (boy did she like Prince's "Head"), the Rock and Roll Animal over on WAAF, the Litch down on WPLR, JoJo Kincaid and Sunny Joe White over on Kiss 108, David Allan Boucher on Magic 106, Mark Parenteau, Albert O, Oedipus, Bradley J—those last three were the ones who smoked Bowie's cigarette butt on the air. ("Bowie only smokes about a quarter of the cigarette and the rest gets stamped out. His lips have been *on* this cigarette! There are still molecules from David Bowie!") I remember the songs they brought into my life—I could go through every name and give you three or four songs I learned from them.

My teen hormones were jangled in the exhilaration of the radio—like the subway, it was a live electric wire that could connect you to the place where the music lived, which for me was the city. I first got to know most of these Bowie songs by taping them off the radio, so I'd get the snippets of the next song the DJ faded them into. The final seconds of "Ashes to Ashes" for me will always segue into the opening organ blare of Squeeze's "Tempted." After "Let's Dance," I expect to hear AC/DC's "Big Balls." One song fading into another—that's the DJ's best trick. The cross-fade is as seductive as the songs themselves. Making a song happen, making it go away. Weaving songs together. Changing each song by what you play after it.

The DJ's got true believers and his believers are girls. They're listening to the radio in their rooms and swaying in their underwear. The girls crank the volume. They sigh at his sexy voice. Or at least that's what the DJ hopes. "I got a girl out there, I suppose," he tells himself. "I think she's dancing. What do I know?" Tragic but true: his believer might be an extraordinarily unglamorous adolescent boy doing his homework, using a vacuum cleaner extension as an air guitar. It doesn't matter: the DJ will do a better job if he thinks I'm a dancing girl. You'd think the song might seem dated by now, rooted as it is in the glory days of rock radio when the DJs picked out their own playlists. But nothing's changed except the technological devices. Just change the hook "I've got believers!" to "I've got followers!" and it becomes a case study in social-media syndrome. The DJ sits alone in the dark, addicted to pitiful jolts of validation from random (and probably imaginary) strangers he'll never meet. That can do a number on a brain. This tune was years ahead of its time.

I'm a believer, so like the DJ, I need to be able to fantasize about who's on the other end of that magic transmission without being troubled by reality. The DJ isn't going to ruin things by intruding on your real life. I remember my favorite DJs' names, but I never google them. I'd rather not see their faces. I'd rather not know where they are now. I could pass one on the street and never know. Like Major Tom, a radio fan picks up secret signals and falls in love with the secrets. Who can be bothered tuning in Ground Control? Turn on the radio and you can get a message from the Action Man. Being a Bowie fan made you feel connected to all the dancing girls out there who were listening to the same DJ, the same station, the same song.

THE DJ IN THIS SONG IS NEVER A CLUB JOCK—HE can't be in the same room as his believers, or any other people, or there's no song. (Same goes for "Last Night a DJ Saved My Life." If the DJ can see she's there, the song doesn't exist.) In my thirties I started following club DJs, but that's a very different devotion. They're there, you know? The club DJ can tell if the song is bombing or if the girls showed up. But the radio DJ has to believe. We need the radio DJ to worry nobody's tuned in—not tonight, maybe not ever. The club DJ sees who's on the floor, how they're dressed, how drunk they are, if they brought a date, if they like this song, if they're cool. The radio DJ has no way of knowing if I'm cool or not. She can't tell if I'm old enough to get into a club. The radio is a place where strangers can meet in the dark and share music.

I discovered college radio DJs, left of the dial. A totally different kind of fandom. MTV arrived and I spent hours every week with all five VJs, got to know their faces, the different music they liked best. Mark, Alan, Nina, Martha—I still thrill to hear their voices on satellite radio (Triple J, RIP). MTV constantly played Bowie, including the "DJ" video, where he wanders the streets of London by night, and people on the sidewalk say "Hey, there's David Bowie" and try to kiss him while he just keeps lip-syncing. At the end of the clip, he spray-paints "DJ" on the glass booth—his initials. I tuned in to MTV to see the world premiere of the "Let's Dance" video, and the "China Girl" video, and the "Modern Love" video. I loved every VJ ever, except Dweezil Zappa.

Being a club DJ was too nerve-racking for me—too easy to keep peeking at how the music was going over, check if any girls were dancing, and it stressed me out. I couldn't handle the peaks and valleys. Much more fun to be a college radio DJ, in the booth, in that room full of vinyl. I used to do an annual Bowie Marathon show on WTJU, and every year the same woman would call in to request "Candidate (Demo)." She's the whole reason I know and love the song. Jeanine got me into "Janine." Ashley is why I know "All the Madmen." Sarah gave me "Watch That Man." These girls would call to ask for their songs. (At least I think they were girls. What do I know?) A woman who gives you a Bowie song is a woman to remember.

The DJ has to piece his personality together, one record at a time. His sexual identity is constantly in motion and it's all guesswork and it's never more than four minutes away from collapsing. After every record fades out, he has to start from scratch. A series of shocks, until he falls apart. He's out of breath from running around the studio, pulling out records, cueing them up—he's out of breath before he even starts singing. Bowie strains his voice in a fit of hysteria, like he can't keep up with all these identities crowding in on him with each single he spins. He's in love with his believers, but he has no idea who we are. The DJ never knows for sure. Bowie was all about eroticizing what you don't know for sure.

THE LODGER

Of all the faux Bowies, only one ever fooled me, and that was
M, who hit Number 1 in 1979 with a new wave electro-disco
anthem called "Pop Muzik." New York, London, Paris, Mu-
nich, everybody talk about pop muzik! A mysterious figure:
nobody knew a thing about this M, or as Casey Kasem called
him, "the man who bills himself as the thirteenth letter of the
alphabet." But my eighth-grade self heard "Pop Muzik" and
knew it was Bowie, putting on the world with this secret identity. Who was he kidding? My friend Flynn and I talked about
it like he was insulting our intelligence with such a transpar-
ent disguise. We weren't even the least bit proud of ourselves
for figuring it out; we thought this was an easy one. I'm not
sure when I decided M was not Bowie—he had his own album
that fall called *Lodger*, with the single "Boys Keep Swinging," much freakier than "Pop Muzik." I no longer knew who
M was (turned out to be a London producer named Robin

Scott—he took the name from the Paris Metro signs) but I no longer suspected he was the former David Jones.

Lodger has to be Bowie's most underrated record. I'm biased because it was the one that came out after I'd gotten into rock radio and become a big Bowie fan, so it was the first new Bowie album I was excited about. "Boys Keep Swinging" was huge for me—it made a mockery of the whole idea of boyness, like a *Mad* magazine parody of Thin Lizzy's "The Boys Are Back in Town." He sang it like a recruitment ad to sign up for masculinity—"You can wear a uniform! You can buy a home of your own! Learn to drive and everything!" Bowie was a boy, but he also sang like a girl, the kind of girl you read about in new wave magazines. Was this a total joke, or only a half joke? Was he suggesting that being a boy and being in drag were the same thing? Was he making fun of boys or coaxing me to see humor in the fact that I had to be one? Was "other boys check you out" gay? Was "you'll get your share when you're a boy" his feminist critique? Did the hook "when you're a boy" mean being a boy was something temporary, a switch you could turn on and off, a mood you could be in when you didn't feel like being a girl? Where was he in this? And where was I? He sang it wearing a skirt on *Saturday Night Live*. The whole performance seemed to say, *this* is what it's like when you're a boy. Good luck, kid.

In the video, Bowie parades down the catwalk in various shades of drag, saying good night as a stern old Marlene Dietrich dowager who blows a kiss to the camera. "Boys Keep Swinging" was never one of his biggest hits, but it's had a notable afterlife. Susanna Hoffs did it brilliantly on her first solo album after leaving the Bangles, *When You're a Boy*, singing it totally straight, even the line "Life is the pop of the cherry." It also kicked off *How to Be a Man*, a very odd CBS prime-time special from May 1985, hosted by Bob "Captain Kangaroo" Keeshan. It was kind of a *Free to Be You and Me* special about gender roles, featuring celebrities like John Denver, Susan Anton, Hal Linden, and Scott Baio in sketches about male stereotypes. The opening number: former teen heartthrob and *Solid Gold* host Rex Smith sings "Boys Keep Swinging" totally deadpan, in front of a chorus line of dancing studs.

As a postscript to "Boys Keep Swinging," there's also the great documentary *The Nomi Song*, about the life and death of Klaus Nomi, who joined Bowie for that famous *SNL* appearance. Nomi and Joey Arias were his backup singers that night (the performance was taped in advance, not live) for "Boys Keep Swinging," "TVC15," and "The Man Who Sold the World." It set new standards for how much musicians could try to get away with on *SNL*, as they performed the songs with avant-garde theater routines involving marionettes, Dada costumes, drag, and toy dogs. Tragically, Nomi was the first noted pop musician to die of AIDS, in August 1983. (It was the top

MTV News story that day, so I spent an entire afternoon hearing Alan Hunter say "coming up, the death of a pioneering new waver" twice an hour.) After his moment on *SNL*, Nomi spent the rest of his life hoping he'd get another chance to team up with Bowie on nationwide TV; he pined away waiting for that lightning to strike again. As with so many Bowie fans, what he learned from the master was how to turn loneliness into a grand theatrical gesture—how to turn your loneliness into a work of art.

Bowie kept toying with gender in outrageous ways, which was the main reason he had left the other 1970s rockers in the dust at this point—he was the only old guy as weird and rebellious and exciting as the new breed. He plucked his own ideas back after they'd been heisted by the punks and the New Romantics. For the "Ashes to Ashes" video, he dropped by the Blitz, the London club where Boy George was the coat-check kid (with a Bowie-worthy rep for picking the customers' pockets) and Visage's Steve Strange was the door guy. Bowie recruited a few of the New Romantic scenesters to appear in the video, including Strange. "Bowie was the reason we were all there anyway," Boy George said in 1999. "The Blitz was a homage to what Bowie had created. So it was fair enough if he came in and said, ooh, I'll have some of that!"

You can hear that insurrectionary gender-fuck spirit all over *Scary Monsters*, where he mixes up futuristic androgyny and rock menace, out-screeching Robert Fripp's guitar in "Fashion" and "Teenage Wildlife." The Bo Diddley groove "Up the Hill Backwards" offered a fatherly pep talk—most likely to his real-life son, in the aftermath of the bitter divorce from Angela Bowie—that advised sensitive young people not to take the insanity of the universe so personally, because "it's got nothing to do with you." He also made the charts with his camp finger-snapping Freddie Mercury throwdown "Under Pressure"—it doesn't sound much like anything else Queen or Bowie ever did, so even though it's one of the most popular tunes by either artist, it's oddly disconnected from the rest of their careers. (Not a lot of flutes on Bowie records.) You know it's a strange duet when Bowie can sound like the mature voice of reason.

"Cat People (Putting Out Fire)" was an even better radio hit, teaming Bowie up with Eurodisco god Giorgio Moroder; the average Bowie kid in 1982 might have been very surprised to hear that in the future, everybody in the English-speaking world would know "Under Pressure," and hardly anyone would give a toss about "Cat People." Blame the *Let's Dance* remake, which has about one-third the juice of the original seven-minute single. But it's a perfect goth-lounge ballad of seething sexual rage, especially in the climactic shriek, "I've been putting out . . . fire . . . with *gas-o-liiiiiine*!" (Quentin Tarantino uses this moment wonderfully in his World War II fantasy *Inglourious Basterds*.) It was the theme song for the quintessential eighties new wave horror movie, starring Nastassja Kinski as a shy Catholic girl who transforms into a bloodthirsty black panther any time she feels the stirrings of lust—what a metaphor for adolescent hormonal confusion. There's terror in Nastassja's eyes and trembly lips when she realizes that she's cursed with too much erotic vitality to join the human race, and that her sex drive is a destructive feline force that will destroy anyone she touches. A very Bowie kind of angst. Trying to make sense out of the libido? It's like putting out fire with gasoline.

THE MODERN LOVER

1983

"Modern Love" is one of those songs I first heard in a record store—it came out during spring break, and as a high-school geek in suburban Boston, my idea of the perfect day off was to take the Red Line into the city and hang out in record stores, flipping through the racks, not even buying them (albums were expensive) but soaking up the knowledge, breathing in the experience of being in the same room as all these LPs and fans who bought them. It was the Strawberries on Newbury Street—they put on the brand-new Bowie album, *Let's Dance*, which I was hearing for the first time along with most of the others in the store. "Modern Love" had an astounding effect on the room—so many people looking up from their browsing, nodding or smiling, even making some eye contact, as if to say, "Are you hearing what I'm hearing? Is it just me or is this song rather quite excellent? Is it going on for another chorus? Three more choruses? Church on time? Church on time!"

I became convinced that "Modern Love" was my new favorite Bowie song ever, a statement of career-summing wisdom,
an opinion I held strongly all year long. My radio was already
swarming with Bowie disciples, from ABC to Duran Duran
to New Order to Prince, and he'd been paying attention; he
covered a great song ("Criminal World") by synth pop Bowie
clones Metro, whose Peter Godwin had a splashy faux-Bowie
hit that year with "Images of Heaven." He even described the
staging of the Serious Moonlight tour as "a slight parody on
all the New Romantics." For new wave kids like me, the idea
that Bowie wanted in on our moment was mind-blowing—
kind of like hearing Marvin Gaye drop "Sexual Healing" and
realizing he'd been studying Depeche Mode and the Human
League. Bowie even brought in producer Nile Rodgers, who
was at a hipness peak, thanks largely to the English bands who
told anyone who'd listen that they just wanted to copy Chic—
especially Duran Duran, who were just breaking in the U.S.,
and who boasted their goal was to combine Chic with the Sex
Pistols. Who could blame Bowie for wanting to join them? After all, Chic and the Pistols both took plenty from Bowie.

Let's Dance was Bowie's pop smash, wearing straight
clothes but still in costume—as Rodgers summed it up, "His
seemingly casual appearance was actually the flowering of his
next drag: He was delving into the eighties metrosexual world
of high fashion, a precursor to what's called 'Executive Real-

ness' in vogueing competions." It was a commercial block-
buster that introduced Bowie to a new generation of American
kids via MTV, who flipped for the "Let's Dance" video and
then went back to catch up on his previous incarnations. MTV
began broadcasting in 1981, in the lag time between Bowie albums, but it was a Bowie shrine from the start. He'd done more
than anyone to insire the visual/musical/sartorial language of
music videos—and Bowie-smitten new wavers were the first
artists who bothered making them. (MTV clichés like "rock
star pouts through window blinds" or "glass shatters in slow
motion" looked cool because Bowie made them look cool.) So
he was a king moving into a castle he'd inspired his followers
to build for him. I watched MTV to catch the world premiere
of "Let's Dance"—hmmm, he looks great, nice hair, stand-up
bass, "put on your red shoes and dance the blues," great line,
okay now we're in the Australian outback, she's trying on red
shoes that don't fit, this is some kind of symbolism, isn't it?
I also tuned in for the premiere of "China Girl"—a satire of
the delusions and dangers of sexual obsession. Actress Jee Ling
stars as the object of desire whom Bowie can only see in terms
of his own masks. It climaxes in a sex scene on the beach—
censored by MTV, who didn't care to display Bowie's ass, God-
given or not.

It's a controversial album in retrospect—the moment where
he gave up experimenting and went pop. It's gotten unfairly

lumped in with later eighties flops, so it's probably worth pointing out that nobody was mad at *Let's Dance* at the time. Whether we liked the new songs or not, fans saw this new smoothie as a role Bowie was playing; we assumed he'd go on to something different next year. The Serious Moonlight tour was his first in five years, and while it wasn't his sharpest band, it was far from a safe greatest-hits revue—song for song, possibly the strongest set list of any Bowie tour. ("Red Sails," "Breaking Glass," "Scary Monsters," "What in the World," "Life on Mars?," "Stay"—those were just the deep cuts.) The backstage photos from L.A. give an idea of where the Thin White Duke's head was at. There's a priceless pic where he sits on a banquette dandling Bette Midler on his lap, squeezed in right beside Michael Jackson (dressed down in shades, blue jeans, dark blazer), and Cher. Bette has this expression on her face that says, "Yeah, this is kinda strange being the fourth-craziest person in the room." Over in that corner: our old pal Henry Winkler. Over there: it's Jaclyn Smith, the Charliest of Angels. If you can't see any humor in the image of Bowie crooning "Station to Station" to the cast of *Charlie's Angels*, it's hard to guess why you'd be a Bowie fan in the first place.

Again, we assumed this was a new role he wanted to play for a while. We weren't so spooked when he insisted this was the *real* him, the one he planned to be from now on. He'd said things like that before. But he did go to extremes in 1983 to stress how normal he was. "I promise you it won't be a cheap shot show," he said. "I won't be trying to put on any pose or stance. You won't see Mr. Iceman Cometh or weird Ziggy or whatever. I was just gonna be me, having a good time, as best I can. And it's working. It's working. It's great. It's terrific. It's given me a whole new audience. It's given me people who, before, would have said, oh, he's that red-haired faggot, you know, we don't want that, we can't see that creep. Now it's changing. Now they like it. That's terrific."

Alarming words, particularly since his fans did not want to share him with homophobes or creepophobes. There's a touch of "come on, it's not that bad" cynicism in his tone. And the f-bomb is grating from an artist who'd proudly identified with f-bombs and other persecuted outcasts. What, he was afraid of ridicule from the straight world now? It was a little late for that. (Stevie Ray Vaughan, who played on the album, left the tour complaining Bowie was "telling us to dress up onstage like fairies.") If the music he made next had been a little better, it'd be easier to hear *Let's Dance* for what it is. But instead, he turned into that wax museum in the desert.

LET'S NOT DANCE

1984–1987–1996

If Bowie had died at the same age as his friend John Lennon—at forty—he would be remembered very differently. It was an all-time low for him. His new album, released in 1987, a few months after he turned forty, was no *Double Fantasy*. *Never Let Me Down* was easily the worst album he'd ever released and his second turkey in a row, after 1984's *Tonight*. Just four years after *Let's Dance*, when he was the elder statesman of rock cool, he had turned into one of those franchises churning out big-budget product nobody paid any attention to. And he'd bailed on the music. As Bowie admitted, "I was letting the guys arrange it, and I'd come in and do a vocal, and then I'd bugger off and pick up some bird."

Bowie spent a decade or so in limbo, still respected for his past, but not for his current music. After the pop glories of *Let's Dance*, he immediately began a long phase of *Let's Not Dance*, and squandered years of hard-earned mystique. Even his sense of style deserted him—the video for "Day-In Day-Out" was embarrassingly long and pompous, where the intro would make you groan, "Oh no, this one goes on *forever*." His major creative project was his Pepsi ad, where he danced with Tina Turner and sang "Modern Love," except he rewrote the words so they were now about Pepsi: "Now I know the *choooiiice* is *miiiine*!" I caught that Pepsi ad on MTV just once, late at night in 1987. It wasn't a controversial sellout—nobody bothered to get mad. It didn't matter enough.

Tonight was a career-freezing disaster, the first record that felt like he was going through somebody else's motions and not even getting that right. He rushed it out a year after *Let's Dance*, which means it was bought on faith by hordes of his new young fans, which means he picked the worst possible moment to suck. *Tonight* should have had a lot going for it—a great trash-rock single in "Blue Jean," a funny harem-pants video, a glossy cover shot of Bowie in blueface. But for never-explained reasons, he didn't keep working with Nile Rodgers—he picked some other producers, nobody in particular, just ordinary eighties producers. Most of the songs were bad cover versions, five of them Iggy scraps. We all got it the week it came out—in September, back-to-school time—and asked each other, "Where the hell is the beat? Where is the modern love? Where is the Bowie?" My freshman roommate, Phil, used the blue sticker that came with the LP to adorn his boom box, where it looked cool—Phil was the biggest Bowie fan I'd ever met. But we only played *Tonight* a few times before going back to our regular diet of *Purple Rain* and *1999*.

Beyond "Blue Jean," the only highlight is the title song, a deeply weird remake of an Iggy death dirge, which he turned into expensively mediocre synth-reggae with Tina Turner. "Tonight" is about mourning a dying lover, so it really isn't the kind of song that demands a perky marimba solo. But the ghastly production just increases the poignance—when Bowie gulps "I will see you in the sky tonight," you can hear real despair in his voice, and the fact that it's buried in so much studio goop gives it more pathos. It sounds numb, which is how grief often feels. (And structurally, it brings back the first verse at the end, which Iggy and Bowie's 1977 original should have done.) I have always doted on "Tonight" as one of the great lost Bowie tracks, but I have to admit there aren't more where it came from—just one moment of Bowie remembering how it felt to be the guy in "TVC15," watching helplessly as something he loves flies away from him, although in this case it might have been his inspiration.

1984 was pivotal for music, with young bands moving in on the arty Bowie kids—the Smiths and the Cure and Depeche Mode on one hand, R.E.M. and the Replacements and Hüsker Dü on the other. Prince dropped *Purple Rain*, an album that consummated everything *Let's Dance* promised, though his guitar sounded more like *Scary Monsters*—Prince now owned the crown. The movie even had the same plot as *Ziggy Stardust*, except with a happy ending where Ziggy/Prince swallows his pride and makes up with the band, i.e., agrees to play one of Wendy and Lisa's songs. He also woos a rebel-rebel muse with the superbly Bowie-esque name Apollonia. Every corner of pop was booming, from metal to disco to hip-hop to Lionel Richie (whose smash ballad "Truly" still sounds to me like a thinly veiled tribute to "Life on Mars?"). Everybody on the radio sounded like a Bowie fan—Cyndi Lauper, Madonna, Michael Jackson, Van Halen, Duran Duran, even his onetime protégé Bruce Springsteen—except the man himself. His most inspired producers were thriving elsewhere—not just Nile Rodgers but Tony Visconti, who recalled, "I made one Adam Ant album and that was my big contribution to the eighties, I guess." (He's being modest—he also produced Haysi Fantayzee's new wave classic "John Wayne Is Big Leggy.")

The fall of 1984 was also when the previously unfindable Velvet Underground records got reissued, which meant most of us finally got to hear them. Lou Reed took over the elder-statesman role. Bowie's best song in this period was a throwaway: "Dancing in the Street," his 1985 forehead-to-forehead dance-off with Mick Jagger, a benefit for Live Aid. Mick and David crashed out the video in one long all-nighter, and it's comedy gold. The two prize peacocks of rock and roll battle it out, shamelessly parodying each other's moves. Bitchiest moment: Bowie totally reads Mick's jazz hands. Funniest moment: while Bowie sings, Jagger leans over to grab his beer off the floor, guzzles it, then fixes his hair. Bowie did "'Heroes'" at Live Aid, wearing an impressively vertical quiff; he got his hair done for the occasion by Freddie Mercury's boyfriend. His most lasting work in this phase proved to be *Labyrinth*. Believe it or not, he was widely mocked in 1986 when he took on the bewigged role of Jareth the Goblin King in Jim Henson's kiddie movie. It looked like the final indignity. But Bowie had the last laugh, because *Labyrinth* became his *Yellow Submarine*—the gateway drug that keeps introducing him to new generations of young fans. At this point, a sizable percentage of his audience probably discovered him as the Goblin King.

BY ALL ACCOUNTS, THE LATE EIGHTIES WERE WRETCHED years for his personal life. His elder half brother Terry Burns had been readmitted to Cane Hill Asylum after years of decline, finally killing himself in 1985 at forty-seven. Bowie avoided the paparazzi-plagued funeral but sent flowers with the message: "You've seen more things than we could imagine but all these moments will be lost, like tears washed away by the rain." The mad brother he'd feared turning into was also the person who'd first given him the hunger to create art—but though Bowie was finally getting paid like a proper rock star, he couldn't ignore what was happening to his art. The Tin Machine project was at least an effort to wrench himself out of his lethargy, but with a supporting cast who didn't sound qualified to function as a backup band, much less as the democratic unit he wanted them to be. His next few records were nice tries—his heart was in the right place, it was execution that was the problem. His skills had just gotten too soft to write new songs. "Jump They Say," a 1993 single, was a heartfelt response to Terry's death. But it looked like Bowie's best moment of the nineties was going to be his funny cover of Morrissey's "I Know It's Going to Happen Someday," which he called "my imitation of one of the great Bowie imitators."

Outside got hyped as Bowie's art comeback: an Eno reunion, a concept album with a plot. It was bought unheard by fans (there were no radio hits) who wanted him back as an edgy artist, now that the 1990s Britpop explosion—Suede, Blur, the Auteurs, Pulp, Oasis, the whole lot—had made him once again the artist every upstart tried to copy. *Outside* was difficult to follow the first time through, but fans persevered because it was Bowie and they really *wanted* to like it. The album has its moments (especially "No Control"), but sadly, judging by the way it dragged down his next few albums commercially, it's fair to say consumers felt burned after a few listens—not just that they'd bought a dull new Bowie project, but that they'd made an emotional investment in an obviously well-intentioned album that nonetheless did not repay close listening the way they hoped it would.

What was going on with this guy? It was hard to tell, all through his forties. He was more beloved than ever, though his new music had no impact at all. He looked divine posing for photos with Pulp's Jarvis Cocker, who presented him with one of his many Lifetime Achievement Awards. He was excited about his Web site. He had shiny new teeth. He'd become one of those Thanks for the Memories guys, which wasn't really the kind of artist he'd ever wanted to be. His pop albums were Bowie trying to guess what might be popular; his art albums were Bowie trying to guess what might be cool. But these albums were neither popular nor cool. It turned out nobody wanted to hear Bowie sound unsure of himself. Nobody held it against him. He'd given the world enough.

LOOKING FOR
SATELLITES

1996–1999–2003

Bowie married Iman in 1992, and it wasn't a big news story. The rocker/model thing had been done a time or two before. However, Bowie fell in love, and this marriage changed everything about his story. It gave him new confidence and enthusiasm about life; it gave him something to sing about. After a few years with Iman, he began writing great songs again, with zero fanfare or acclaim, and never made a lazy record for the rest of his life. He was inspired as a writer again, because he had found a reason to care: marriage, the grand theme of his golden years. The cliché about how rock stars write all their good tunes when they're young and miserable, then they get happy and go soft? And their sober family-man music is a bore? Another cliché Bowie decided to destroy. He is the prime example of a rock star who found the right muse and slowly got his mojo back. Iman got him to the church on time.

For the last few years of the eighties, he was dating Melissa Hurley, a young dancer from the Glass Spider tour—in the show, her routine was pretending to be a random fan pulled out of the audience, à la Springsteen's "Dancing in the Dark" video, then they start to tango and by the end of the song her legs are up on his shoulders. Just from watching her in the Glass Spider video, she seemed too warm and vivacious to be paired with a figure as tired and listless as Bowie was at the time. Iman, to those of us reading gossip magazines in the checkout aisle, seemed a better match. She had her own money and her own career. She also clearly had a mind of her own. They'd both go into this with their eyes open and the paperwork in order. We hoped they'd get a few pleasant years before the lawyers got called in, everything civilized, and then maybe he could marry Winona or somebody.

When they wed in 1992, Iman was on MTV more than he was, thanks to her role as an African queen in Michael Jackson's "Remember the Time" video. (A superb comic performance, with Eddie Murphy as her king and Magic Johnson as a court slave.) The Somali model was always a mysterious figure—she came too early for the fashion-mania of the nineties, too grown-up and severe to fit in with the *House of Style* craze. Iman wasn't in the George Michael "Freedom! '90" video. Bowie met her in 1989 and fell in love instantly. It took her time to reciprocate, but he wooed her—he had never publicly talked about any romantic partner with the ardor he had when raving about Iman. The marriage lasted over two decades, till death did them part. Bowie was one of those rockers (Paul McCartney and Simon Le Bon and Lou Reed come to mind) who adapt easily to marriage because by the time they settle down they've exhausted every imaginable sexual curiosity and there is nothing left to tempt them. Threesomes involving alpacas and bathtubs full of Camembert? Bowie left that behind in some hotel room way back when. It was like the old song he'd cut with Lou Reed, "Hangin' Round": "You're still doing things that I gave up years ago." He had his eyes on a romantic adventure he'd never experienced, one he knew he wouldn't get another shot at, and it transformed him in ways a fan wouldn't have dreamed possible. When they married, Iman was probably the only person who believed he had it in him.

I got the *Earthling* advance cassette in the mail, in November 1996, and popped it into the boom box. My expectations were low, to say the least. The press release said it was his drum-and-bass album—how sweet, just a couple years late. I was perplexed at how convincing it sounded right away—these were real songs, under those annoying but easily ignored snippets of dated techno percussion. He announced his seriousness with "Looking for Satellites," easily the strongest song he'd written in a decade and still for my money the peak of his nineties. For that song, Bowie went to the mirror he always faced to size himself up: outer space. The exuberance of the music was contagious. "Dead Man Walking" (about going down the aisle) and "Battle for Britain" (about getting scared at the idea you can never go back to the loser you were before you met her) were on the same level, facing up to slippery feelings beyond the ones he'd addressed on *Low*, as in the way he sang lines like "Catch the last bus with me / Give the last kiss to me." You could hear it in his melodies; you could feel it in his voice. He was excited about these songs.

Earthling and the next record *Hours* were so damn good, it was startling to hear them, but it was tough to convince my friends they were worth getting excited about. Bowie had squandered most of his fan-excitement capital with the hoopla for *Outside*. For a rock critic trying to spread the word, it was also a tough sell to my editors, let alone readers, that "Bowie's jungle album" was not his jungle album at all but his "Bowie writing real songs about real stuff and meaning it" album. Of course I used the line "his best since *Scary Monsters*." Virtually every critic did, even those who didn't like the album much. I wanted to say "his best since *Let's Dance*," but my editor convinced me I was the only one who considered that a compliment. *Hours*, packaged as "Bowie's R&B album," went equally deep. "Seven," "Survive," and "Thursday's Child" felt like Babyface and Toni Braxton doing *Young Americans*. The major flaw of these records, one that many listeners understandably found (and still find) impossible to get past, was the butt-ugly guitar sound of Tin Machine leftover Reeves Gabrels, which was even more irritating than the techno effects. It would have been great to hear Bowie redo these songs with a better band and better production. I played them a lot anyway.

Earthling and *Hours* weren't even revivals of his earlier inspiration—they were something new. Hardly anyone noticed. This music didn't fit anybody's narrative of what Bowie stood for or why he mattered. The rock audience of the late nineties was bigger and more voracious than ever, buying new music in a consumer frenzy that would peak at the turn of the century, but Bowie wasn't part of this boom. *Hours* was his first album in twenty-five years to miss the Top 40 of the American chart. If these records had been debuts from some new English band, they might have gotten more love—they would have been Spacehog, at the very least. It evidently didn't matter much to him. He tossed the Lifetime Achievement tiaras aside and went back to work. There weren't any more hits—he was done looking for those, no longer pushing through the market square. He had nothing to prove—just something to sing about.

He took his enthusiasm on the road, touring hard with a drastically upgraded band—exit Gabrels, enter Earl Slick and Mike Garson, along with fantastic bassist Gail Ann Dorsey, as word finally started to spread about the roll he was on. He kept giving his albums anti-mythical one-word titles: his next were called *Heathen* and *Reality*, enhanced by the change in guitarists and even more by the return of producer Tony Visconti, with spiritually questioning songs like "Sunday" and "Slip Away" reflecting his life in New York as a husband, dad, and man about town. I saw him at Madison Square Garden in December 2003, one of the great rock shows of my life. At one point he stood there, basking in the audience rapture, and politely asked us all to give him one more big scream. Everybody screamed. Bowie bent over in half. "Excuse me," he said. "I've just come."

ALL THESE YEARS OF LIVING IN NYC, YOU'D THINK I'D have an "I met Bowie" story, instead of merely offering my friend Jenni's, but man oh man is it a good one. It was early 2007. She was out in the East Village on St. Mark's Place in the middle of a blizzard, trying desperately to hail a cab. So he was the only other pedestrian on the sidewalk. When a lone pair of headlights finally appeared through the snow, the stranger gallantly said, "Go ahead." She said, "Why don't we share?" He helped load her shopping bags into the trunk. It was only in the cab that the scarves and hats came off and she said, "Oh, I know who you are." She made the split-second (but brilliant) decision to start talking about herself and tell him her entire life story, so he could relax and not have to entertain this stranger he was trapped with. This was the wise approach—she's a shrewd celebrity whisperer. (I would have asked arcane music questions until he decided to take his chances on hypothermia.) She told him every last detail of her family life ("You've got to forgive, for your own sake," that's what he kept telling her) until the taxi reached SoHo. As she got out, he said, "Now, when you tell your friends about this, make sure you mention that I was wearing fabulous shoes."

Then she went upstairs, took her coat off and called everybody she'd ever met to tell them this just happened, which is why I believe it. So I'm passing it on here. He was wearing fabulous shoes.

WHERE ARE WE NOW?

2004–2013

After his 2004 heart attack, when we all feared losing Bowie for good, he went into an unannounced retirement. The rumors from Ground Control all said the same thing: He's done. He's survived his health scare and changed his priorities. He's being a dad out in the country in upstate New York and living the private family life he missed out on before. Happy as a clam. No desire to go near a stage. Not even writing songs for himself. No statements about retiring—that would just invite attention. Won't return calls from his own office. He made all the music he needs to make. He had that life already. He's done.

Bowie wasn't a recluse—he took care to show up in public often enough that nobody could accuse him of being in hiding, a smart way to avoid "Is Bowie Alive?" headlines and paparazzi. Yet he chose very sporadic and tightly controlled moments to appear—introducing Ricky Gervais at a 2007 Madison Square Garden show, a Sundance red carpet for the 2009 premiere of his son Duncan Jones's film *Moon*, singing "Fantastic Voyage" with Alicia Keys's band at a charity gala in New York, a cameo on a TV on the Radio album. He made his last high-profile concert appearance in May 2006, at a Royal Albert Hall show in honor of his old hero Syd Barrett. He joined Pink Floyd's David Gilmour for two songs: the cross-dressing ditty "Arnold Layne" and a classic from *The Wall*, "Comfortably Numb." Bowie sang the verses, confirming the song as the "Space Oddity" sequel it always was. ("Helloooo? Is there anybody in there?") As Gilmour took over to sing the chorus, Bowie discreetly backed away from the lip of the stage. By the closing guitar solo, he had mysteriously vanished into the night. The lodger had checked out.

So the shock was real when he returned with *The Next Day*—an announcement on his Web site on his sixty-sixth birthday that he had an album of new songs on the way, with a preview, the ballad "Where Are We Now?" I reviewed the album for *Rolling Stone* in February 2013, which meant going to listen at the office of his publicists. There were just two CD copies of the album in existence, one in Europe and one in America, both under constant guard. It was one of those security situations where you're alone in a conference room with the CD; I wouldn't have been surprised if someone was checking through a two-way mirror to make sure I didn't turn on my phone. I liked the first song a lot—but oh, the second song.

"The Stars (Are Out Tonight)," it was called. I got to the end of the album, then played this song four times in a row. I asked myself, "Is it unprofessional to get up and dance? I mean, if any security guys are watching, would I traumatize them?" I got up and danced. This was Bowie's best song since "Modern Love," which was thirty years earlier. Like all his great songs of his final decades, it's about how weird it feels to be in love for (and with) the rest of your life. I scribbled the lyrics in my notebook so I could read them to my wife over dinner. Bowie was taking me to the church on time, one more time.

In the conference room I looked out the window at the night sky, selfishly playing the whole album a third time. It was almost 9 P.M. I'm sure his publicists wanted to get home. I listened to "Where Are We Now?," name-checking specific places he remembered from Berlin, though I have never been to Berlin and my images of it come mostly from Bowie records. He keeps singing about "walking the dead," as if it's like walking a dog—you take your collection of ghosts for a walk, when they insist on it, and you revisit the places you shared. You return to those places and times in your mind. Or maybe you even physically stroll through the city and let the ghosts reaccess it through your living eyes. Like another song set in Berlin, "'Heroes,'" it's about respecting a temporary moment of human fellowship and resisting the temptation to make it fraudulent by pretending it can or should last forever. You take your dead friends for a walk, spend some time together, then they move on.

It reminded me of one of my favorite Lou Reed songs, his 1982 ballad "My House," another song about being haunted by a dead friend (Lou's college poetry mentor Delmore Schwartz). Like Bowie in 2013, Lou in 1982 was a happily married man, and who knows, maybe the fact that he was deeply in love was one of the reasons the dead friends kept coming back to visit, as if to share a bit of that human warmth. Lou Reed was still alive in February 2013; so was David Bowie.

THE BLACKSTAR

1947–2016

TEN

Bowie released "Blackstar" in November 2015, with no advance warning: just here it is, the new ten-minute Bowie song, with an album on the way in January, but meanwhile it'll take you a couple of months to wrap your head around this track. "Blackstar" was an astonishing song: a slow-burning torch ballad, as he sings about returning to outer space, the place he always goes to ponder basic Bowie concerns like love and death and the terror of knowing what this world is about. The song unfolds for ten minutes without sounding forced, mixing up Coltrane's *Olé* and "Planet Rock" beats, as he sings, "I'm a blackstar. I'm a blackstar."

He released the album *Blackstar* on his birthday, January 8, a Friday, and for a couple of days it was the new Bowie album. It seemed like most of my friends spent the weekend playing it, even friends I thought weren't into music anymore. My wife and I played it over and over; although we'd already loved the title track for a couple of months, it sounded even more massive now. One of his best songs ever, we agreed—a weird enough idea to compute. By Monday morning, *Blackstar* wasn't his latest album anymore, but his goodbye album. The songs now had all these new stories in them. The final song, "I Can't Give Everything Away," was now his last word. As Visconti said, it was his "parting gift."

The whole album was a love letter he left behind for everyone, talking to us about what he was going through, giving us music to grieve with, so we could feel closer to him as we went through the shock and bewilderment of his death. He'd spent all these years building a unique connection with his fans, and now he'd spent his final year making a soundtrack to the bereavement he knew was waiting for us. He sang about his grief and fear, his pain about the people he was leaving behind. In "Blackstar," he sings the key line: "At the center of it all, at the center of it all, your eyes."

The world responded—*Blackstar* became his first U.S. Number 1 album. Everybody went back and watched the video he made for "Lazarus." Bowie in a sickbed, eyes bandaged, singing "I've got scars that can't be seen." Bowie writing at his desk, nodding off asleep, fighting to stay upright. Bowie wobbling across the floor and locking himself in the cupboard.

NINE

He and Iman got twenty years together. They deserved fifty more. They fell in love at a time when he was wiped out as a musician, and her love gave him his music back, which gave Bowie back to the rest of us. A real-life adventure, worth more than pieces of gold.

In the millions of conversations I had about Bowie the week he died, people kept saying how grateful we all were to Iman, yet realizing we didn't know her very well; her personality always seemed reserved and unimpressed by the celebrity dazzle. None of us had ever seen a single photo of their teenage daughter.

EIGHT

Bowie's space songs were always about isolation and his desire to overcome it. In 1972, he said "Starman" had "the immediate level of 'There's a Starman in the Sky saying Boogie Children,' but the theme is that the idea of things in the sky is really quite human and real, and we should be a bit happier about the prospect of meeting people."

That's clear in "Blackstar," as he fades into the sky, no longer visible from earth but still there.

SEVEN

In the early years of his marriage to Iman, Bowie got his first tattoo ever, on his calf, as a symbol of his love for her: a dolphin.

SIX

Sigmund Freud gives the classic definition of how grief fucks with your brain, in *Mourning and Melancholia* (1917): "It is a matter of general observation that people never willingly abandon a libidinal position, not even, indeed, when a substitute is already beckoning to them. This opposition can be so intense that a turning away from reality takes place and a clinging to the object through the medium of hallucinatory wishful psychosis." In other words: David Bowie's entire career.

You see something, you fall in love with it, you invest your libidinal energy in it, and then when it dies or leaves you, you go a little insane, you redesign your concept of reality so you can keep loving it awhile longer. You keep hanging on.

FIVE

All over *Blackstar*, you can hear Bowie tip his fedora to musicians he'd given birth to. "Lazarus" sounds just like the Cure circa *Disintegration*, with that Robert Smith–style guitar. "Dollar Days" swipes a hook from Morrissey (the "Jesus made me so" bit in "November Spawned a Monster"). But before *Lazarus* came out, Visconti revealed that Bowie's main inspiration was Kendrick Lamar, who made everybody's favorite album of 2015, *To Pimp a Butterfly*. You can hear that in the leisurely jazzy grooves of *Blackstar*. The music sounded nothing like *The Next Day*, which was full of short punchy rock songs.

Bowie listened to Kendrick and got an idea for a different way he could approach music. He still wasn't finished learning.

FOUR

"Blackstar" uses "Planet Rock" beats—and of course, there's a long story encoded in those beats. Afrika Bambaataa's 1982 hip-hop classic "Planet Rock" sampled the synth hook from Kraftwerk's 1977 electro classic "Trans-Europe Express," the song where they gave a very German shout-out to Bowie: "From station to station, from Dusseldorf city / Meet Iggy Pop and David Bowie." *Station to Station* was already heavily influenced by the Kraftwerk album *Radio-Activity*, which built on the hazy cosmic jive of "Starman." The Morse-code piano hook in "Starman"—that comes straight from Diana Ross and the Supremes' "You Keep Me Hangin' On," the 1966 classic from the young black Americans at Motown. The beat goes round and round, from station to station, and you can hear that story in the music.

Bowie's love connection with hip-hop has always been a fascinating thing. The Roots' Questlove has a funny story about playing the Public Enemy album *It Takes a Nation of Millions to Hold Us Back* for the first time in 1988, hearing that "Fame" sample, and saying, "Wait, that's my *sister's* record collection." Bowie was the rock guy in 1983 who stuck his white neck out and said that yes, he wanted his MTV, but he wanted to see more black artists there. He definitely wasn't the only MTV fan who felt this way, but it took an artist of his visibility to risk saying it out loud—at a time when he was promoting a new record and had something to lose. (And it was very much to MTV's credit that they put Bowie's words on the air.)

A 2005 TV ad for XM satellite radio: Snoop Dogg can't find his beloved gold chain. Where is it? He wanders through the XM studios, asking the celebrity DJs doing their radio shows. Nope, Ellen DeGeneres hasn't seen his chain. Neither has baseball star Derek Jeter or country singer Martina McBride. "Hi, Snoop," Bowie says, sitting in his DJ booth under the "On Air" sign, playing some sitar music. He gives an innocent shrug and shakes his head, sending Snoop off with a black-power salute. Then Bowie leans back in his chair with a mischievous grin. He's wearing the Snoop chain. The music we hear: "I am a DJ. I am what I play."

THREE

Sometimes an artist makes an album, then dies, and everybody decides the final album has all these premonitions on it. But *Blackstar* is different because it's the death letter of an old man who unambiguously did not want to die. It was important to him to make that absolutely clear in his final music. He wanted more time. He had more records he wanted to make. Unlike some other artists who've knowingly made their goodbye albums, like Johnny Cash or Warren Zevon, Bowie wanted to keep his terminal illness private as long as he could, so he could keep it in the family. He couldn't give everything away.

After his death, Visconti explained how Bowie eventually had to tell the musicians who played on the album about his cancer, because he couldn't hide that he'd lost his hair. Everybody who played on the album knew what was going on, and none of them betrayed the secret.

TWO

Bowie spent much of his final year working on a project that seemed like an unusual choice for him, the musical *Lazarus*. It had a limited run that winter, in a tiny theater in the East Village. Seats were sold out long in advance, mostly to the theater's season-ticket holders. I saw it on December 3, with three friends from *Rolling Stone*; we went in the afternoon and waited in the box-office line a few hours before the doors opened, figuring if somebody didn't show up for their season-ticket seats, the theater might release them at the last minute. We went on a Tuesday; that seemed the likeliest bet. Plenty of people lined up behind us. We got lucky—four seats were empty, two of them together, so all four of us got in, a few minutes before curtain. I sat right in front of Anna Wintour and Idris Elba. Not a jukebox musical, not many hits. The audience was mostly elderly theater people, not a rock crowd or a Bowie scene; people perked up at "Changes" and "'Heroes,'" but not "It's No Game" or "Always Crashing in the Same Car."

Lazarus picked up the story of *The Man Who Fell to Earth*—all these years later, the Bowie spaceman is still stuck here, a rich and miserable alcoholic, played by Michael C. Hall from *Dexter*. He meets an angel, a teenage girl, and she becomes a daughter figure to him, renewing his desire to live. She helps him build a spaceship so he can finally go back to his home planet. *Lazarus* is full of images you'd only recognize if you know the movie inside out—for instance, there's a snippet of "Hello Mary Lou." But the audience was clearly touched, even when the story got obscure, like the scene when the spaceman's personal assistant sings "Changes" while raiding the refrigerator in lingerie and throwing glass bottles across the room.

The Bowie spaceman builds his rocket ship. The love of his angel daughter has set him free. He blasts off at the end. Before he goes, they sing "'Heroes'" together. The finale is intensely moving. Milk spills all over the floor (angel blood, they called it) and the Bowie spaceman swims like a dolphin. Really—he jumps down on his belly and does the dolphin swim across the floor, through the milk puddle, his arms stiff at his side. She laughs and joins him. They sing the lyrics with a slight tweak, on the "because we're lovers" line: "We're free now, and that is a fact."

They swim like dolphins, and when the song is over, he flies up into the sky.

ONE

My birthday came in early February—a big birthday, a round number—and my wife and I celebrated with a long-planned trip to Joshua Tree, hiking the Mojave Desert and driving around to the Bowie CDs we burned. (Left them all behind by mistake in the rental car. I hope the next driver enjoyed them.) The night before my birthday, we drove out to Pappy & Harriet's Pioneertown Palace, a roadhouse in an otherwise empty stretch of desert. It was open-mike night, a Monday tradition there. When we walked in, a country singer was onstage doing a song we recognized: "Wild Is the Wind." "I guess Johnny Mathis did that song first," he said. "But I think David Bowie got it from Nina Simone." We got a table facing the stage, ordered ribs and beer and cheese fries. The next song he sang was a country classic, Keith Whitley's "Don't Close Your Eyes."

A rockabilly trio was up there, backing the people who'd signed up to perform. Some folksingers, a few old blues harmonica guys, a ukulele girl, a jazzy saxman, two guitar boys in Nirvana shirts playing a Beatles song. A clutch of crusty hippies got up to sing "Lean on Me," reading the lyrics off a phone. The MC knew all these folks, sat in with a few of them. Then the MC started strumming a riff and announced, "Some of you are probably too young to know this song. But this one goes up to the king." Then he sang the words, "I will be king," and everybody in the room replied, "And *youuuu*. You will be *queeeen*." The night turned into a Bowie jam-session sing-along dance party, because of course it did. Everybody who brought an instrument hopped onstage; the rest of us were out on the floor. Harmonica Joe was wailing away. I got a snippet of phone video, but I couldn't show it to anybody, because it's ruined by the sound of my voice screaming "I remember! Standing! By the wall!"

They played "Ziggy Stardust," though nobody could remember the words to the "some cat from Japan" verse (except a couple of strangers on the floor, dancing in the dark). The MC wanted to close out the night with "Starman," but the band didn't know it, so they just played Neil Young's "Like a Hurricane" while he sang "Starman" over it. They fit together perfectly.

I will never see any of those people again, but I will remember them, and we can be heroes, forever and ever. Just another group of strangers he assembled, touched with his presence, and then sent on their ways to scatter around the world. The world is full of us. And that means the world will always be full of David Bowie.

ACKNOWLEDGMENTS

This book was Carrie Thornton's idea, and she's the one who believed it was possible. She called the morning after Bowie died and asked, "Can you write a book about him in a month?" I said, "Well, he made *Low* in a month." Thank you, Carrie. Thanks to all my friends who helped and inspired me, knowingly or not. If you and I know each other, we've probably talked Bowie, and your enthusiasm is probably in here, smiling and waving and looking so fine. So thank you.

The people who helped on purpose were many, especially Daniel Greenberg. Thanks to all at Dey Street Books, particularly Lynn Grady, Sean Newcott, Michael Barrs, Tanya Leet, Joseph Papa, Nyamekye Waliyaya, Andrea Molitor, Elsie Lyons, and Jessie Edwards. Darcey Steinke, Abbie Jones, and Elizabeth Mitchell for our Bowie memorial dinner. Abbie again for schooling me to the resonance of *Labyrinth*. Gavin Edwards for wisdom. Ultimate Bowie scholar (and fellow *Earthling* fan) Andy Greene, Alison Weinflash, and Annie Licata for *Lazarus*.

I couldn't have written without Sean Woods, my wise and inspiring editor at *Rolling Stone*, and all my *Stone* colleagues past and present, especially Jason Fine, Nathan Brackett, Jon Dolan, Christian Hoard, Brandon Geist (for trading emails about Bowie and Lemmy at 4 A.M.), Hank Shteamer, Gus

Wenner, #BrittanySpanos, Simon Vozick-Levinson, Brian Hiatt, Jason Newman, David Browne, Mikal Gilmore, Patrick Doyle, David Fear, Kory Grow, Suzy Esposito, Jon Bernstein, Peter Travers, Coco McPherson, and Jann S. Wenner.

Thanks to Marisa Bettencourt for the fly photo. Caryn Ganz, for breaking the news in such a merciful way. Jenni Lee, for her taxi story. Will Dana, Maria Sherman, Erica Tavera, Joe Gross, Sean Howe, Joe Levy, Matthew Perpetua, Marc Spitz, Jonathan Lethem, Pam Thurschwell, Lisa Randall, Robert Christgau, Jenn Pelly, Marc Weidenbaum, Jeffrey Stock, Stephanie Wells, Phil LaMarr, Jill Mapes, Chuck Klosterman, Liz Pelly, Phil Dellio, Jen Sudul Edwards; Strummer and Dashiell; Drema, Ruby, Simon and Buddy; Brian Morgan and Holly Porter-Morgan; Ted Quinn and everybody at Pappy & Harriet's Pioneertown Palace.

This book is dedicated with love to the passionate bright young things in my life, my nieces and nephews, who might drive their mamas and papas insane but make their uncle feel very lucky. Crazy love to my whole family, especially my sisters Ann, Tracey, and Caroline; my brothers John, Bryant, and John; my parents Bob and Mary Sheffield; Donna, Joe, Sean, and Jake Needham; Jonathan, Karianne, Ashley, and Amber Polak; Tony and Shirley Viera.

The biggest love and loudest thanks imaginable to Ally for being my hero.

NOTES

These are the key books I relied on while writing. First among equals is Nicholas Pegg's *The Complete David Bowie,* which has never been more than a few inches from my nightstand in the past fifteen years. (Right now as I type, I have the 2000 edition next to my bed and the 2011 edition on my desk.)

THE TOP TEN:

David Bowie and Mick Rock, *Moonage Daydream.* Universe, 2002.

David Buckley, *Strange Fascination.* Virgin, 1999.

Kevin Cann, *David Bowie: A Chronology.* Simon & Schuster, 1984.

Kevin Cann, *Any Day Now: The London Years, 1947–1974.* Adelita, 2010.

Simon Goddard, *Ziggypedia.* Elbury, 2013.

Chris O'Leary, *Rebel Rebel: All the Songs of David Bowie from '64 to '76.* Zero, 2015.

Nicholas Pegg, *The Complete David Bowie.* Titan, 2011.

Thomas Jerome Seabrook, *Bowie in Berlin: A New Career in a New Town.* Jawbone, 2008.

Mark Spitz, *Bowie: A Biography.* Three Rivers Press, 2009.

Hugo Wilcken, *Low.* Continuum, 2005.

ALSO CRUCIAL:

Chris Adams, *Turquoise Days: The Weird World of Echo and the Bunnymen.* Soft Skull, 2002.

Nina Blackwood, Mark Goodman, Alan Hunter, and Martha Quinn with Gavin Edwards, *VJ: The Unplugged Adventures of MTV's First Wave.* Atria, 2013.

Harold Bloom, *Kabbalah and Criticism.* Continuum, 1975.

Victor Bockris, *Transformer: The Lou Reed Story.* Simon & Schuster, 1994.

Roy Carr and Charles Shaar Murray, *David Bowie: An Illustrated Record.* Eel Pie, 1981.

Simon Critchley, *Bowie.* Or, 2014.

Geeta Dayal, *Another Green World.* Continuum, 2008.

Sean Egan, *Bowie on Bowie.* Chicago Review, 2015.

Tony Fletcher, *A Light That Never Goes Out: The Enduring Saga of the Smiths.* Crown, 2012.

Chet Flippo, *David Bowie's Serious Moonlight.* Dolphin, 1984.

Sigmund Freud, *Mourning and Melancholia,* in *The Standard Edition of the Complete Psychological Works of Sigmund Freud,* translated by James Strachey, Volume XIV (1914–1916). Hogarth, 1971.

Peter and Leni Gillman, *Alias David Bowie.* Henry Holt, 1987.

Mervyn Holland, *The Wilde Album.* Henry Holt, 1998.

Dylan Jones, *When Ziggy Played Guitar: David Bowie and Four Minutes That Shook the World.* Random House, 2013.

Kerry Juby, *In Other Words.* Omnibus, 1986.

Nick Kent, *The Dark Stuff.* Da Capo, 2002.

Nick Kent, *Apathy for the Devil.* Da Capo, 2010.

Sean Mayes, *We Can Be Heroes: On the Road with David Bowie.* Independent, 1999.

Jimmy McDonough, *Shakey: Neil Young's Biography.* Anchor, 2002.

Barry Miles, *Paul McCartney: Many Years from Now.* Owl, 1997.

Kenneth Pitt, *The Pitt Report.* Omnibus, 1983.

Thomas Pynchon, *Gravity's Rainbow.* Penguin, 1973.

Jonathan Rigby, *Roxy Music: Both Ends Burning.* Reynolds & Hearn, 2008.

Dave Rimmer, *New Romantics: The Look.* Omnibus, 2003.

Mick Rock, *Glam! An Eyewitness Account.* Vision On, 2006.

Nile Rodgers, *Le Freak: An Upside Down Story of Family, Disco and Destiny.* Spiegel & Grau, 2011.

Paul Roland, *Cosmic Dancer: The Life and Music of Marc Bolan.* Tomahawk, 2012.

Ken Scott with Bobby Owsinsksi, *Abbey Road to Ziggy Stardust: Off the Record with the Beatles, Bowie, Elton & So Much More.* Alfred, 2012.

Slash with Anthony Bozza, *Slash.* HarperCollins, 2007.

Paul Stump: *Unknown Pleasures: A Cultural Biography of Roxy Music.* Thunder's Mouth, 1998.

Elizabeth Thomson and David Gutman, *The Bowie Companion.* Sidgwick & Jackson, 1993.

Paul Trynka, *Starman.* Little, Brown, 2011.

Tony Visconti, *Bowie, Bolan and the Brooklyn Boy.* HarperCollins, 2007.

Steven C. Weisenburger, *A Gravity's Rainbow Companion.* University of Georgia, 2011.

Also countless issues of *Rolling Stone,* right up to recent features by Brian Hiatt and Andy Greene; *Mojo,* especially Paul Du Noyer's "Contact" from July 2002 (Du Noyer's superb website has full transcripts of his interviews); and *Uncut,* especially Chris Roberts's "Gimme Your Hands" from March 2003. Also *Q, Select, Melody Maker, NME, Record Mirror, Spin, Creem, Crawdaddy, People, Playboy, Modern Drummer, Musician, Billboard,* and *Black Collegian.* The 2004 *NME Originals: Glam* has been committed to memory for years now.

The Boston Phoenix is archived on Google Books—to read Mike Freedberg's "Dream Lovers," click on January 24, 1984, and scroll to page 39. Unwieldly but worth it, I promise. Here's to the fan websites Teenage Wildlife, Bowie Golden Years, Bowie Wonder World, 5 Years, and More Dark Than Shark. Chris O'Leary's blog Pushing Ahead of the Dame has been part of every Bowie freak's life for years now; the book version, *Rebel Rebel,* is even better.

I've also relied on my own *Rolling Stone* interviews with Brian Eno, Iggy Pop, Nick Cave, John Taylor, Nick Rhodes, Karen O, and the goddess Stevie Nicks. Thanks to all.